The Servant Warrior

The role of faith in law enforcement

by Kevin McInnes

Produced by:

FriesenPress
Suite 300 – 852 Fort Street
Victoria, BC, Canada V8W 1H8

www.friesenpress.com

Distributed to the trade by The Ingram Book Company

Table of Contents

Acknowledgements

In any major project, there are always a number of people that help you get something done. First of all, I need to thank Jason Bradley from Red Deer River Ranches in Sundre Alberta, for allowing me to stay at the ranch for a month with my two boys. Jason put us to work but gave me free use of a cabin to begin my writing. What a blessing this was to all three of us.

Secondly, I need to thank all the police officers and their spouses across Canada that gave me their time, thoughts and experiences to help me in researching this book. In particular, I need to mention Chris Butler, Terry Larson and my partner in chaplaincy and crime and good friend, Jim Amsing. Each of these men gave me a great deal of insight into their world and helped me with the content, editing and commentary on the subject matter.

I would also like to thank Kathleen Mailer for her encouragement to continue with the publishing process and the encouragement needed to get this book on track and to print. Thanks to Nik Dominique for your setting up of the book.

Katherine Matiko did the editing of this book and worked her fingers off for me. She read and reread, edited, gave me suggestions and encouraged more stories, then reread it again with more editing. She honoured my story and edited this out of the goodness of her heart. Katherine, Thank-you so very much.

Jeanette Sthamann saw a vision for the Servant Warrior and the result was the front cover of this book. I am deeply indebted to her visionary mind and artist skills. Wow.

I need to thank all of my children because they put up with their Dad who was learning both how to be a parent but also to be a parent who's a cop. They put up with a lot of police personality stuff but I am grateful to God above for the way they have all grown into wonderful children and adults in whom I am well pleased. Christa and Lindsay, in particular, had to put up with my role while I worked the street and put up with night shifts and being interviewed and a tired Dad. You girls are truly my young princess warriors. To Adam and Alex, my young servant warriors, for our time out the Ranch and the chats we had under the stars. The beginning of this book with you boys is a memory I will forever cherish.

Of course, behind every good man is an even greater woman so my deepest thanks goes to my Princess Warrior Deborah who has loved me with intent and encouraged me to write this book. I can assure you that without her this book would not have happened. She has believed in me and stood by me when I wanted to quit. Thank-you for loving me through the difficult years when I was trying to find out who I was. Thank-you for staying with me when I did and it wasn't that pretty.

Finally, my thanks is to my God who loves me and called me into His ministry to officers and their families. He alone kept saying, "Finish your book." He has given me an identity, says he's proud of me and given me a task in this life that I could not have imagined or dreamed. He is faithful.

The Servant Warrior

Introduction

Why did I write this book? To show that being a police officer and a person of faith within the career is completely compatible, contrary to how many people have viewed faith and policing. Most people see faith in policing as a weakness not a strength, a crutch not suitable for a strong, macho person who must control all situations and be in control of him or herself. I disagree with this very strongly and I wanted to show that a person of faith, particularly in the God of the Bible, is in fact seen by God as highly favoured, honoured and loved. This is a powerful strength if seen in the right context.

In preparing for this book, I interviewed many officers and their spouses across this country of ours. I could not have done it without their honest answers to the questions I asked. Most of the officers and spouses I spoke with had many years of experience in policing. Some had very opposing views about our roles as police officers. Most were married and some had experienced divorce and its pain and remarried with a newer philosophy. From their answers, I gleaned information that would help me understand how faith played or didn't play a role in their careers and how it affected their marriages if at all. This information I have passed on to you, the reader.

I wanted to show through the Bible that God also gives us direction on how we are to do the work of peace officers. We are to be both a servant to the public, which must remain confident in us, and a warrior who stands in the gap between the poor, oppressed and victimized and the evil that seeks to consume or destroy them. As police officers we are also in a position of leadership. Citizens are looking to us for leadership. Our own peers are looking for leadership and chances are becoming a leader will be a reality in many people's careers. The Bible gives us direction on what kind of leader we should be and gives a good example of that leadership. I wanted to look at that example and find principles of leadership that can encourage officers to be led well and to lead well. Regardless of our position in our careers, we will be always be under the direction of another. I believe that to be a good officer requires that we learn to be under submission with properly understood humility.

We can also receive good instruction on how to be a whole person within the context of policing, which means we must look after the relational, physical, emotional, spiritual and intellectual parts of us. Historically, we've done a good job physically and intellectually but we don't do so well with the emotional, relational and spiritual sides of our being. Once again there is good instruction in the Bible to guide us.

Finally, I wanted to address one of the most attacked areas of policing and that is marriage. In the United States, police marriages rarely survive and in Canada, it's only marginally better. My discussion is admittedly only a beginning but I wanted to address some issues that were identified and some principles that can perhaps instill some sense of hope in the police world of marriage. I've tried to distill some of the principles I learned from other officers whose marriages have worked and what they did to survive and thrive in a culture that can destroy marriage if we let it.

I hope you will enjoy this book. Mostly, I hope you will see the love that God has for us through His son, Jesus. He loves us, has called us, has equipped us and has given us principles under which we can guide our lives and our careers. In doing so, we learn how to serve the public better and fight evil with courage and diligence. We can do this with a deep sense of purpose and calling and also know that our most important relationships can really be the rocks on which we build a solid career and life. May God bless you as you pursue one of the most important callings God can give anyone. Love God and love the people you serve.

Kevin McInnes

Chapter One
My Story

I was raised in a Christian home by parents who were Salvation Army officers. They both understood the role of service in their lives and gave themselves to it fully. My parents never really fought in front of us children. I never knew what domestic violence was. Occasionally, when I was a very young boy, intoxicated strangers would come to our door looking for hand-outs from the Salvation Army, hence my parent's house. I remember being a bit nervous about that but our dog Goldie, a Labrador retriever, would ensure my parents' safety. I'd never seen or dealt with a hooker, a drug addict, a dealer or a biker. If I had, I certainly knew nothing of them or their lifestyle. Needless to say, my life was quite sheltered and separated from many of the vices of this life.

With my parents being Salvation Army officers, we moved many times across Canada. I came to love this country as I learned a great deal about the different cultures in Canada. From Newfoundland to Quebec, Ontario to the West, there is a great deal of variety in the way people think and relate to each other. Our moves provided many points of connection with people as my life progressed. If someone you dealt with knew you were from a certain area, it often brought commonality and allowed opportunities to build relationship and dialogue. This would become important to me later on.

My wife and I were married in Montreal, Quebec in 1977 and a year later moved to Calgary, Alberta. I had been pursuing a career in the teaching profession in physical education at McGill University. However, due to the political climate in Quebec under the Levesque government, English schools were becoming an endangered species. Job prospects for an English-speaking teacher would be limited at best. Consequently, my wife and I moved west with hopes of finishing school in Calgary. I took a job with a major bank, hoping to pursue my education once we were settled. That never happened until many years later and in an entirely different field.

I quickly learned that banking was not my forte. I did not enjoy being inside leading a fairly inactive life behind a counter or desk. I was bored and looking for excitement.

From the time I was eighteen years old, I believed that my "calling" was to be a minister, to follow in my Dad's footsteps into the Salvation Army. I continued to explore that but the timing didn't feel right then. I knew I needed to change jobs. I wasn't happy. My younger brother applied to the Calgary Police Service and was not accepted because of his age. I was two years older so I figured I might give it a shot. I had no *calling* to policing at the time but it sounded exciting, it was outside and more active. I would be helping people and I could do that until I went into the Salvation Army. I applied to Calgary Police Service in September 1979. On November 19, 1979, I was sworn in as a full-fledged police officer, vowing to serve and protect the public with my life if necessary.

It didn't take me long to realize that I was in way over my head. Oh, training was fine and really quite a bit of fun, but I was different. As far as I could tell, I was the only "Christian" in the class. If there were others, no one was saying. I began to think perhaps this police work and being a Christian wasn't such a good idea. I did meet a gentleman through church who'd been with Calgary Police Service for a number of years but left to go to Alberta Highway Patrol. He made it very clear to me that it was impossible to be a cop and a Christian. The lifestyles were just too incompatible. It wasn't long into training that I began to wonder if that wasn't really true. Perhaps they didn't belong together.

I was now hearing about the "us vs. them" mentality; the "Pucous Delectus Supremous" who were out to kill me and my peers. I needed to watch my back and my partners' backs all the time because there were people out there waiting to kill a cop. I had to be wary at all times, vigilant at every call and determined not to believe anything without proof.

The happy day came when I graduated from police college and was posted to one of the tougher neighbourhoods in Calgary. God and the leadership of the training section were good to me and put me under the tutelage of Sgt. Barry Davis, a Christian cop. So they did exist! To this day, I credit Sgt. Davis with my survival as a police officer. He mentored me and introduced me to other Christian officers through the Fellowship of Christian Peace Officers. This gave me hope. Not much, mind you, but some. My first year was spent having my wits scared out of me and not having a clue what I'd gotten myself into. Between dealing with hookers who smashed up clients' houses over not getting paid, to biker gangs blowing each other and their club-houses up, I began to learn what it meant to be a cop—but more importantly, a Christian cop trying to live by the ideal of serving others in a way that represented Christ in a very broken world.

I now saw firsthand how police officers coped with the lifestyle. Some drank excessively, some chased women or men as their next prize, and others were experiencing divorce, usually because of the first two. Mostly, they were cynical, angry individuals who seemed to avoid dealing with people and their problems. I wasn't coping much better either and anger seemed to be the way that I dealt with most things.

My wife Deborah saw this but didn't realize that it was the job. She thought it was her and I didn't know enough to tell her otherwise as plainly as she needed. I was trying to survive. Don't get me wrong, I had learned to love the job. Despite how we as officers coped, we did it together; often we had a lot of fun and really enjoyed catching the bad guys. It was exciting. From night shift boredom—driving around an industrial area where the only moving objects were our vehicle and the rabbits we were chasing—to exhilarating foot chases with would-be break and enter artists, I came to love policing. My identity began to revolve around, "I am a cop." <u>BUT</u> the question remained, "Could I be a cop and a Christian?" Were they compatible? After all, I had just been told by another young officer that he wouldn't work with me because I was a Christian. He was concerned that if push came to shove, I wouldn't shoot. My naïve Christian lifestyle was seen by many as a "fatal" weakness.

About two years into my career, I had the opportunity to work in another area of the city, closer to where I lived. I was able to work with some excellent officers and continued to mature as a police officer. I started becoming more comfortable with who I was as a cop. Soon I was working with some partners—one in particular, Len Grenier—with whom I was catching bad guys on a regular basis. This became addictive and eventually my reputation as a decent cop began to override my "weakness" of being a Christian. The District (Division) I was in started a new youth program and I was recommended by my supervisor for the position. I worked with four other officers in a team. Here my confidence grew tremendously as did my skill level in investigations under the tutelage of an excellent supervisor, John McKinnon. Eventually my partner Rick Weafer and I received a Deputy Chief's compliment for a series of ten major investigations we completed.

After I left the youth program and went back to the street, I worked with some excellent partners. One such partner, Rene Lafreniere, had the reputation of being heavy-handed and had been to Internal Affairs a number of times. We were put together (I was senior to him) to help calm him down. Rene and I fit like two peas in a pod. Rene was a big man, much bigger than me, but he was truly a gentle soul inside. He clearly used his size to his advantage but never once did I see him do anything untoward to other people. He and I received a couple of Senior Officer's recognitions for our investigative work, once clearing 27 house break-ins against four accused.

As my career progressed, my Christian "weakness" became much less of an issue and my ability as a police officer grew. I was placed on several specialty teams, supervising some, and was given the opportunity to act in a detective role on many occasions for over a year without the promotion. Out of this came several more senior officer compliments and another Deputy Chief's award for cracking a multi-million dollar theft ring operating in Calgary and internationally. Numerous arrests and convictions were obtained.

I was a cop and it was a blast. My thoughts of ministry had been put to rest. Deborah no longer felt that she could do ministry training and raise children at the same time resulting in some difficult personal struggles between my wife and me, so I thought policing was it. I focused all my attention on getting promoted to detective. I had a supervisor supporting me wholeheartedly and I had the examples to support my calling. Sadly, I lacked one thing. I was not well known to those making the decisions. I even had my detective trainer comment on my evaluation that I needed to become more politically known if I was to be successful.

After five promotional exams, four attempts, one near miss and the final blow of being ignored, my aspirations of becoming a detective took a serious blow. What I didn't know at the time was that God knew I was going in the wrong direction. He had called me into ministry when I was eighteen and He was serious about it. What I didn't know is that He was redeeming my situation and leading me to ministry.

Due to a series of personal crises involving my marriage, my church and now my work, I had lost hope and felt betrayed and abandoned. I gave serious thought to suicide and had the tools to carry this out. During this time, I had given so much attention to the promotional process that I caused my wife to feel forgotten and unloved. She was now third place, at best, and was lost in my desires for promotion. This led to some very difficult communication barriers for both of us and each feeling a deep sense of loneliness.

I was an elder at our Church during this time as well. The church was going through some serious growing pains and had lost of few of its leaders. Down to a few of us, we were being asked to make a decision around a salary increase for our pastor that did not sit well with me. I objected, creating a wall between myself and the pastor, resulting in my stepping down from leadership. I felt betrayed and alone in this as well compounding my sense of hopelessness and worthlessness. I truly wondered where God's love for me was. I did not see it in any of the areas of significant meaning to me.

Thankfully my wife was a praying wife and we had a miracle holiday worthy of another story and I sought the counseling that I needed. After six months of counseling, a short stint on anti-depressants, a renewed sense of who I was truly in Christ, and a deeper sense of Deborah's love for me and me for her, I began the slow process of healing. I changed the focus of my career and went into the School Resource Officers program. I loved it. I was teaching, having a positive effect on students, parents and staff. I was coaching, doing outdoor education and fulfilling my dream of being a teacher.

God was still not done. A personal friend, Dave Dyck, was aware of my desire to finish my degree, this time in religious studies. Out of his generosity I was able to start back to Bible College. Shortly after, the Lord began to reveal His next plan for my life. One of our officers, Rob Vanderweil, was killed in a traffic stop by an ex-cop from Jamaica. A large police funeral was held, the first I had been involved with as a member. I didn't realize it at the time, but Rob Vanderweil was a classmate and friend of Jim Amsing who would later become my partner. Jim was a pallbearer and intimately involved with that funeral.

A year later, Rick Sonnenberg was killed by a young offender driving a stolen car in excess of 160 kmh. Rick's body exploded on impact as he was trying to lay down a spike belt. This happened in front of his partner who was helpless to do anything about it. I knew both Rick and Lisa Schirok as teammates and was, like everyone else, devastated by what happened. The funeral was held at the Jack Singer Concert Hall because it was so large.

When all was said and done, some officers and one of my supervisors came to me and said I needed to seriously consider police chaplaincy. We had a chaplain at the time but it seemed to some of us that he did not understand our culture well. I presented a plan to the Calgary Police Service who, unknown to me, was planning changes to our Employee Assistance Program. In October 1995, I became one of only three serving police officers in Canada who were police chaplains. The other city was Winnipeg whose program we modeled.

Within weeks of my appointment, Cst. Jim Amsing and I met for the first time formally and discovered a mutual desire for chaplaincy. So began a partnership which exists today. My calling had been irrevocably changed. Instead of a calling within a religious setting, I was now called as police officer/chaplain in a secular setting.

During this period of time, my wife and I seemed to be having this calling confirmed in our lives as a couple. Our purpose, in particular, was becoming clearer. From the time of our marriage vows, Deborah and I felt that God had called us for a unique ministry but we really had no idea what it was. We'd tried many different things in our search but the role of chaplain began to make things clearer.

As part of my education, Deborah and I attended a week-long conference dealing with the spiritual disciplines. We hardly spoke to each other during most of the training, which was done in silence. However, as we left the retreat centre, we asked one other what we had heard from God. Both of us were convinced that our ministry was to peace officers and their spouses and families.

In our years as husband and wife, we knew firsthand the struggles that follow those in law enforcement. Marriage is not easy when one partner witnesses violent deaths, hostility and events most people run from, while dealing with people who want to kill them because of the uniform. As an officer I watched many of my peers contend with broken marriages, divided families and the pain that went along with it. Others struggled with addiction to prescription medication or alcohol (particularly early in my career) and occasionally drugs. Sex was another addiction I observed in some partners caught up in the "blue fever" (women in love with the uniform).

As the chaplain, I now became much more involved in the critical events that our officers faced. These included shootings, death of children, death of our own officers through tragic events, death of family members and much more. I became much more aware of the spiritual needs of our members.

Over the years I began to observe that although spirituality was still resisted there was an increased willingness to at least discuss it. I also discovered there were many more officers of faith than would actually say so publicly. Privately, they would attend church but publicly say little if anything about their spiritual journey. I also began to discover that frequently it was the senior officers who had been through the struggle of the profession that were more open to discussing spiritual matters. Perhaps they had discovered that the macho image and tough exterior had not served them as well as they originally thought it would. I frequently learned of retired members who did not attend any religious gathering during their careers but who were returning to church afterwards as if it was now OK to do so. The old saying, "You can't be a cop and a Christian," was being lived out after retirement for when they were no longer cops they could pursue faith.

There aren't many books or presentations in the law enforcement field that look at the role of spirituality in policing. My hope is that by putting my thoughts to paper, new and veteran officers will see the direct benefit of a faithful expression of their chosen profession. Faith will actually strengthen their ability to perform the job of law enforcement. There is no weakness involved if faith is properly lived out.

God has provided a special calling and provided the authority and power, both legally and spiritually, to perform our duties. We truly are God's servants as well as servants to the public when we serve faithfully. God is also a warrior and leads us in battle against evil. We too are warriors called for purpose and there is much instruction for those who wish to be faithful servant warriors.

My hope is that the reader will see value in the term "servant warrior" to describe the role of a peace officer. Faith can provide a significant foundation on which to build a solid and successful career.

Chapter Two
The Servant Warrior's Identity

Who are you, Mighty Warrior? This is a question that has been rolling around in my head for some time. So much of our identity as individuals, particularly as men, is dependant on what we do. In a recent conversation, a gentleman was telling me how he responds in conversations with others. He never brings up the work that he does but waits to see how long it takes for someone to ask him what he does for a living. He is rarely disappointed because invariably, some will ask soon into their conversation, "So, what do you do (for work)"? It is interesting watching people's expressions when you tell them you are a cop! Oftentimes you will get statements like, "Oh, I know a police officer, do you know so and so?" or "I dealt with this cop; he was the biggest jerk ever."

These conversations can lead to defending the actions of another officer to an ignorant member of the public. Sometimes the cop becomes the center of attention and tells numerous dangerous and/or funny stories that his audience seems to lap up. At times the opposite is true. The officer will not say what he does or masks what he does to avoid the usual.

For several years in my early career as a police officer, I struggled greatly with exactly who I was. Was I a cop or was I a Christian or was I somewhere in between? Maybe I wasn't really either but I was just using these terms to clarify what I did or how I lived.

Dr. Kevin Gilmartin in his book *Emotional Survival for Law Enforcement* points out that very often police officers lose their sense of identity because several healthy roles in their lives are distilled down to one which is simply, "I am a cop." He says, "The effects of this over identification emotionally with the police role and the reducing of the sense of self to one dimension have significant impact on the personal and work relationship of the officer in numerous ways. As the officer's sense of self becomes increasingly one dimensional, the officer becomes more at risk emotionally."[1]

I believe that this is a significant reason why I was told in my early career that I couldn't be a police officer and a Christian. Life for some officers had been reduced to the one dimension and only lip service was given to the other possible roles in their lives. Consequently, cynicism breaks into their lives and makes it diffi-cult to see anything other than through the "cop-filter." As I reflect back I would have to agree wholeheartedly with Gilmartin's comment that these officers are most at risk emotionally.

An area of interest for me over the past ten years is in Critical Incident Stress Management. I have attended numerous courses and conferences in CISM. I participated in several group debrief-ings during tragic events. I have learned and observed that a significant critical incident can have an overwhelming effect on our world view. World view can be simply described as the view we take as to how the world operates or should operate. A critical incident can leave some reeling if their world view isn't large enough to deal with evil or if their view of personal safety is forever threatened and altered. This altering can have an impact on personal identity, who they are and what they think they are here for, even whether they will be here long.

A couple of years ago, a particularly tragic event occurred at the Calgary Police Service. One of our tactical officers was shot and killed in a training accident by his peer and friend. This was profoundly devastating for the officer, the TAC team and the Service. World views could have been shattered and I am sure that some were clearly altered; however in the midst of this intense tragedy, several members of the team asked the chaplains to pray, to seek the counsel and guidance of the Creator. Their world view accepted the fact that despite horrendous loss, God was somehow in control. No one understood this tragedy—how could you?—but in the midst of it we sought God and cried out for help.

This accident had a significant impact on how business and training was conducted following the reviews. I know that it forever changed some of the people involved. The faith in God of many involved helped to give a greater foundation for their lives and kept them focused, steady and able to carry on effectively. The expression of faith through prayer, I believe, was able to mitigate the symptoms of those who could have been at significant emotional risk.

Bruce Siddle wrote a book about the science of warrior preparation and training for those in law enforcement. This is in no way a religious book; however at the end of his book he speaks of a supernatural faith that extends beyond this life.[2] His argument was that a warrior needs to have his eternal identity and destiny sorted out prior to getting into a situation where fatal force is required. Not having dealt with this issue could cause an officer to hesitate. That hesitation could have fatal consequences to the officer. A recent written interview with Sgt. Chris Butler of the Calgary Police Service's skills and procedure training section confirms this opinion. "Many police officers that have been in deadly force encounters that have not previously resolved this issue recount having these thoughts enter their minds. The time to start figuring out your mortality is not when someone is trying to kill you.....In the heat of combat when your life is on the line, this question cuts through the fog of battle and suddenly becomes of utmost importance. Much better it is when some one is trying to kill you, to figure out how to solve the problem, rather than reflecting on your own mortality at that point in time."

A very good point. Resolving the issue of who we are relative to God is of vital importance. However, if we do as Gilmartin says and find our sense of self wrapped up in being a cop, our identity is limited and we are at risk.

To that end I would like to suggest that faith is an important component in the role of policing because it helps us establish a healthier sense of identity. Back to the question, "Who are you, Mighty Warrior?"

When our identities are wrapped up in who we know, what we do or have done, or what others think of us, we are on shaky ground. Oftentimes our identity rests on our success. In an excellent book for those facing retirement or beyond, Bob Buford's *Finishing Well* describes an incident where greyhounds were taught to chase a mechanical rabbit to determine the fastest dog. One day, the mechanical rabbit broke down, allowing the dogs to catch the rabbit. This caused a great frenzy at first. However, shortly thereafter the dogs stood around absolutely confused about what to do.[3]

In terms of policing, there is no shortage of "rabbits" to catch. There is always another bad guy to catch, another success on our belt, but sooner or later we wonder what significance is attached to all this. Success has been described as victories won for ourselves. Significance is what we have done for others. More on this later. The point is, success can often leave us feeling empty because it is not lasting. You are only as good as the last bad guy you caught, which others will quickly forget about. If our identity as officers is built on success and our performance, it is doomed to frustration and cynicism.

Faith in God can help combat our issues of identity. When you are aware that a higher being, someone who is infinitely beyond us, values us and has a purpose for us that is far beyond our "rabbits," we can rest on a much firmer foundation on which to build our lives, our families and our careers as officers. When we know that God has a much larger view of the picture than we do, we can know eventually that God is working things out according to His will and purposes. He values us and has a specific purpose and calling for us to complete that will not be forgotten but rewarded eternally. There is hope and significance.

One of my favourite verses in the Bible with reference in particular to peace officers is Matthew 5:9: "Blessed are the peace makers, for they will be called sons (and daughters) of God." The verse generally means that those who pursue peace on this earth will be sons of God. This verse is intended for all those who pursue peace. However, from my highly-biased position as a chaplain and now retired police officer, I argue the verse has specific value to those of us who have pursued peace as a career. We are called the "sons" of God. We are part of God's family where we are and will be eternally significant. Our identity is now found in God and His purposes rather than ourselves and our purposes which can be fleeting at best and quickly forgotten. What we do and more importantly, who we are, have eternal consequences and when we find our identity in God through faith, we are on much firmer ground. Specifically, our role as husbands, wives, fathers, mothers, community members and police officers has value and significance eternally. There is a bigger picture—a rabbit that can't be caught—that gives focus to our lives as officers. I believe that this will combat cynicism and much of the depression that seems to follow officers who have lost their focus. Knowing we are approved of by God makes a huge difference.

It is not an accident that in the Bible, peace officers or those who played a significant role in law enforcement are given a high place of honour. God knows that the identity of peace officers is crucial to their well being. This has not changed over the centuries and millennia. It is still true today. In Jesus' time, soldiers were the law enforcement of the day. To ensure those in law enforcement know they have value and are approved by God, they show up at the beginning of the Gospels with John the Baptist giving them instructions. Jesus pays the highest possible compliment to a centurion because of his faith when the centurion asks Jesus to heal his dying servant. Jesus states he'd seen no stronger faith in his entire ministry than from this law enforcement member. A centurion expresses awe as he witnesses the Son of God die on the cross and recognizes the profound impact this Jesus must have had. The first non-Jewish Christian, Cornelius, was a law enforcement officer who God honoured because of his great faith. The entire story of his conversion is told in the Acts of the Apostles.

I believe this is God's way of saying that 'you are my beloved sons and daughters and to show you, I will give you prominent places in the story of my Son.' It is important also to know that the approval of a father towards his son or daughter is vitally important to a son or daughter. Numerous studies in the sociological and psychological arenas and my personal observation as a police officer have proven that the father's approval gives the child the sense of self worth and value that gives life to that child. Children know their mothers generally love them because of the nurturing and care they give to their child. It is the father's approval that gives identity and self worth. It is this approval that gives strength and courage to become all that we were intended to be. It is this approval that allows police officers of both genders to fully appreciate their identities and truly become servant warriors.

I am not saying that people who grow up without a father who does this in their lives are doomed or that singles moms can't do an effective job of raising children. I am saying that it will be much harder and God gives grace to the fatherless.

Jesus, the Son of God, needed that father's approval as well and it is interesting to note that God, the Father, gave Jesus His approval before Jesus' ministry even began. Just before Jesus begins his ministry, he is baptized by John the Baptist in the Jordan River. At this time, the voice of the Father God is heard and says, "You are my beloved son in whom I am well pleased." Jesus' career hadn't even started yet. All his performances were yet to come. No miracles, no teaching, no healings, no followers, not much of anything really and yet the Father calls out to those that will listen, "I love you and I am pleased!" It's too bad many children do not hear that from their Dads. It has a profound effect. Those that do hear it relish in it. He is about to begin his servant ministry and his Father says 'I approve!'

The same assurance of the Father's love and approval for Jesus occurs again just as Jesus is about to face the most difficult phase of his ministry, one he knows will lead to his own persecution, suffering and ultimately brutal death. Jesus has completed much of his ministry journey around Judea and Jerusalem and his reputation has followed him in every area of Israel. Jesus goes with his best friends to a quiet place where he is transfigured from a normal human to where his heavenly glory breaks out a bit. The disciples watch with utter amazement as his body begins to glow and Moses and Elijah show up to encourage him in this next difficult phase. Once again the voice of God the Father is heard, "This is my Son, whom I love; with Him I am well pleased. Listen to Him." Jesus is about to begin the Warrior's journey into the greatest battle he'd face and the Father says, "I approve!"

The soldiers and centurions mentioned in the Gospels of Jesus show up at the beginning and at the end of His ministry. It is as if God the Father is saying to us, just as He did to Jesus, that we are approved. We are honoured and recognized as significant in God's economy.

Living under the unchanging love and approval of God Himself that is not based on how we perform is an incredibly freeing thing. It is empowering, encouraging, strengthening. We are the Beloved of God. We are His sons and daughters.

I had a partner several years ago who had a faith background but had struggled with it. After his officer coach phase I became his partner. We had a great partnership and a lot of fun together. He never fully grasped his sonship with God, though. Some time after our partnership ended, he found himself in an affair. His marriage failed as a result, leaving several children without close contact with their Dad and a spouse hurt and wounded. Through a series of difficult circumstances for himself, he came to an end where his faith became significant and he began to understand his sonship and relationship with God. Through a mutual friend's counsel and support, this officer understood God's adoption of him as a son and began to live like it. Today he is an outstanding officer and leader. He remarried and has remained faithful and committed to his wife. All this came because he began to understand, through faith, his identity as a son of the Creator.

I can say this also from my own personal experience. With nine years on the job as an officer and many senior officer compliments, I was encouraged to seek promotion to detective. For four years I pursued this and began to place my identity into this basket. In my final year of attempting promotion, I'd had the best year of my career and had been recognized for exceptional work. When my promotion was essentially ignored I was devastated. While there were other issues in my life at the time, this rejection of who I thought I was broke the camel's back and I crashed into a depression and cynicism with the job and management. It took six months, a great wife, a good counselor and a renewed sense of who I really was before I recovered. I placed my identity and meaning back into God's hands. Eventually it led to a promotion of a different kind, becoming the first sworn police officer chaplain in Calgary. I had a much firmer foundation on which to lead my life.

While I will go into more detail on this aspect later in the book, it is important within the context of our identity as servant warriors that we understand what God calls us. Through the Apostle Paul, God calls those who are in law enforcement His "ministers". There are only two callings found in the New Testament that are specifically called ministers. One is those who give leadership in the church and the other is those who give leadership in law enforcement. This is an identity that God Himself calls us to, equips us for and outlines how we ought to do this work. Within the context of our being sons and daughters, we are also given gifts, abilities and purpose as members of the family. In our case it is to be ministers of God Himself as servants and protectors of His people.

The first role of faith in policing is to provide a secure identity on which to build purpose and significance that goes beyond our own personal success and who we think we are. So, who are you,

Mighty Warrior? You are a beloved son or daughter of God if you possess faith. You are a man or woman of eternal significance with a high calling and purpose.

Chapter Three
The Servant Warrior's Purpose

Faith in God provides a significant role in establishing our identity as, most importantly, beloved sons and daughters of God. God provides identity. He provides purpose and calling. There are very few occupations in God's Word where those that serve are specifically called God's servants. One of those occupations is law enforcement.

Before I became a police officer, I had no idea how many references in the Bible pertained to those in law enforcement. After becoming an officer, I began to see that many of the references to law enforcement were extremely complimentary and empowering. Soldiers, centurions (leaders of over 100 soldiers), prison guards and judicial rulers are all described in very positive terms throughout the New Testament in particular.

Peace officer or police officer is a relatively new term compared to the terms soldiers and centurions. Throughout most of history, it was the soldier in various forms who enforced the rules of the land. In New Testament times the soldiers of the day were the police of the day. When a soldier was not engaged in battle for the country or state, he was to work at his posting or home area to assist the community in which he lived. His assigned task was to assist in the infrastructure of the community. Soldiers helped with road construction, bridges, community building and of course the enforcement of state laws.

The centurion was often directly involved with the leadership of the community. He would assist with establishing what infrastructure was required and assign the manpower. He would be the equivalent of a Police Inspector (Canadian terms) in charge of a Division or District. There are several stories in Scripture that refer directly to the role of the centurion in his community. More importantly, Scripture refers to the outstanding faith of these men and the impact that faith had on those around them.

In the Gospel of Luke, Chapter 7, the story is told of a gentile Roman centurion who had a fatally ill servant. He sends some community representatives to Jesus to ask for healing for the servant. This centurion understood authority and submission to it and simply asked that Jesus heal the servant. Jesus didn't need to come but just say the word! This expression of faith astounds Jesus. He had not seen such an expression of faith in all of Israel. This compliment is not paid to any other person in the Gospels, yet it falls on the faith of this law enforcement officer. For me personally, this passage alone gave me great hope that being a Christian and a police officer was very possible.

In the book of Acts, Peter the Apostle receives a very disturbing dream in which he is told to eat food prohibited to him by Jewish law. At this time, the stories of Jesus had not been taken to the Gentiles, only the Jews. Peter is then told to go with men from Caesarea and speak to Cornelius, a centurion of the Italian regiment.

Peter understands the dream then, goes with the men that came at Cornelius' request and presents the story of Jesus to

Cornelius and his family. Cornelius and his family become the first Gentile Christians which opened the door of Christian faith to the whole world. A law enforcement officer became the first representative of Christian faith outside the Jewish world.

Again in Acts, Chapter 16, the Apostle Paul and his companions are thrown in jail for removing an evil spirit from a young slave girl. The owner of the slave girl had been profiting from the girl's ability to tell the future. The owner takes Paul to court and Paul is thrown in prison. While in prison, there was an earthquake that essentially releases Paul and his friends because the doors opened and the chains fell from the walls. None of them choose to escape. The prison guard sees what happens, figures he's as good as dead with his superiors and is about to take his own life. Paul stops him, shares the love of Jesus with him, and the prison guard and his entire family become some of the first converts to Christianity in the City of Philippi.

I tell you these things simply to show that faith, specifically faith in Jesus, and policing is completely compatible and are in fact praised, highlighted and encouraged throughout much of the New Testament.

The Bible has much instruction for officers, some of which I will highlight later in terms of training, family life and personal life issues. For now I would like to focus on Romans 13:1-6 because these verses are very specific to the role of purpose for those in law enforcement.

"*1* Every person is to be in subjection to the governing authorities. For there is no authority except from God, and those which exist are established by God. *2* Therefore whoever resists authority has opposed the ordinance of God; and they who have opposed will receive condemnation upon themselves. *3* For rulers are not a cause of fear for good behavior, but for evil. Do you want to have no fear of authority? Do what is good and you will have praise from the same; *4* for it is a <u>minister </u>of God to you for good. But if you do what is evil, be afraid; for it does not bear the sword for nothing; for it is a minister of God, an avenger who brings wrath on the one who practices evil. *5* Therefore it is necessary to be in subjection, not only because of wrath, but also for conscience' sake. *6* For because of this you also pay taxes, for rulers are <u>servants</u> of God, devoting themselves to this very thing." Romans 13:1-6 (NIV)

From the very beginning of creation and following through the history of man, God the Creator established boundaries for man to live by. In the Garden of Eden the first man and woman were told where the boundary lay. Of every fruit and tree they could eat but of one only they could not. Evil entices all of us and they ate what they were not supposed to out of lies and desire to be like God. Not much has changed over the years.

Throughout the Old Testament, God established laws and ordinances required to allow men and women to live pure and right lives. They would benefit tremendously if they followed His laws. They would have great success in their work, their homes and as a community. The laws were designed to empower people to live valuable and profitable lives, lives in which even their enemies would not succeed against them.

If however people chose, and they did, to disobey the laws, they would face the consequences for those failures. As police officers, we are constantly bombarded by the consequences in people's lives of their failure to obey the laws of the land. All of us in law enforcement can immediately bring to mind difficult and emotional moments where we have seen up close and personal the devastation of broken laws. Even as I write this I am saddened to know that on March 3rd, 2005 four brave RCMP officers lost their lives to a drug dealer and grow operator in Mayerthorpe, Alberta because he and his peers failed to adhere to the laws of our country. Four, really five, families will be reeling from this devastating loss and will not recover for many years. God had warned His people that failure to adhere to rules established for our blessing would result in devastation. As such God has established governments to establish His laws and order for His people. What is interesting about this passage in Romans is that the government at the time was the Romans. The Romans had established a fairly peaceable and economically successful empire mostly because God's rules were being adhered to. However, at the higher levels of government, specifically the Caesars of the day, decadence and immorality became the norm.

At this particular time, Nero is the Caesar. While it could be argued that nationally things were moving along OK, privately and to a larger degree things were beginning to fall apart. Nero began to use Christians as martyrs. He placed animal skins over live Christians and watched as lions ravaged them to death. He put oil over the bodies of people, tied them to poles and burned them alive to be used as street lamps. It is during this time that Paul, writing to the Romans, tells them to obey the government. Generally speaking, God has established government to establish His laws and to care for the needs of the people. Clearly there are leaders of government who do not adhere to God's laws and create destruction for their people. It is interesting to observe history and see that eventually these leaders are overthrown and new governments are established. We all rejoice when good governments rule the people well. When bad government rules, the question of obeying these governments is a lot more difficult. Discussing the theological and personal implications of bad government is really outside of the intent of this book. Having said that, Scripture tells me that God has established all authority, good and bad, for His purposes which are beyond my ability to fully understand. He has also shown in Scripture that those who do not lead the people in right living will be punished themselves and their authority removed. God has placed them in authority for His eternal purposes and designs but woe to those who lead badly and abuse the people. Scripture itself shows God as the warrior, defending the weak, the poor and the disadvantaged.

The laws of this land, Canada, have been established by God through those He has placed in authority over us. The government will be held accountable for decisions which do not line up with the laws of God. It is the responsibility of the people of the land to live in submission to the laws of the land. If individuals choose not to, they themselves will receive judgment for their wrong doing. It is the responsibility of the government, under God's authority, to bring judgment to these individuals.

These verses are so important to those in law enforcement because it clearly defines our purpose and our authority.

Romans 13:3 says, "For the rulers hold no terror for those who do right, but for those who do wrong. Do you want to be free from fear of the one in authority? Then do what is right and he will commend you." As a police officer, if there was one thing that would really upset me, it was when parents, with good intentions I believe, would use us as a threat to their children in our presence. They would say, "If you don't behave yourself that policeman will take you away!" On more than a few occasions I would stop what I was doing and confront the parent. As officers, we need to be seen by young people as a place of refuge and safety, not a place of terror and fear. We are there to help these children, not cause them to fear us. They should fear us no more than they do their own parents, who should be correcting bad behaviour themselves, not using us as a "terror." It is our responsibility to commend good behaviour on the part of our youth and children and encourage them when they are good citizens.

That aside, the definition of "ruler" in this passage refers to all those who are under the authority and direction of the government in relation to the law. This list would include but is not limited to the minister or government representative in charge of law enforcement, judges, lawyers, prison officials, and all peace officers including municipal police, RCMP, Customs, Fish and Wildlife and Corrections.

Rewarding the Good

It is the primary responsibility of this group of individuals to commend those who do what is right. It is our responsibility to encourage, promote and reward good behaviour. For years psychologists have been telling us that if we want to see good behaviour continue, catch and reward people when they are doing something right. This begins with little children we praise like mad when they say their first words or take their first steps, right up to adults we find risking their own lives for the sake of others.

I have had the privilege of being part of a police service that many times has tried to commend those we catch doing right. One of Calgary's officers started a program which was endorsed by the Service to reward and give out coupons for various stores and restaurants to children who were caught doing something right. On occasion our traffic section would stop motorists, not to hand out traffic tickets for violations but because they observed them being good drivers. It is such a joy to stop a friend or citizen, see the expression of concern ("What did I do, Officer, did I do something wrong?"), only to watch those expressions turn to smiles and laughter as rewards and commendations are given out. It is a lot of fun and sure beats dealing with a difficult and rude driver.

As the chaplain for the Calgary Police Service, I have had the great privilege of attending the Chief's Awards Banquet, where members of the public and police were rewarded for their bravery and life-saving tasks. Friends and family, city officials, and senior police leaders all attend. It is a time of celebration and rejoicing with people who understood the right thing to do even if it meant risking their own lives while doing it. My job was to give praise and thanks to God for His covering of safety and for the willingness of people to do right.

A couple of years ago, a young man who owned a security company was swimming with his own children at a swimming pool in Calgary. He was playing in the wading pool when he noticed a small child under the water near where he was. He responded immediately and grabbed the little child. He threw the child over his shoulder and began to push on her chest. The little girl was not responding and not breathing. He ran for assistance to a concession area and asked for the ambulance to be called. Another gentleman, a pastor from Manitoba, came by and while this young man is pushing on her chest, the pastor prayed for the little girl. Within seconds the girl sputtered and threw up water and began to breathe. The parents were located and EMS arrived to confirm the near drowning. It was my privilege to hear this story first hand. People who do these kinds of things need to be commended by the rulers and heroic behaviour supported.

While I have, for obvious reasons, noted one Service, I know that most other police services including the RCMP also look for opportunities to praise those who do right.

While I was a school resource officer at one of our high schools I received the support of many students to begin a program called Lancer Pride. The purpose of the program was to support students who were doing good things for the school and other people. It was to show pride in the great things that our young people are doing in our society and community. This group of young people began doing projects in association with a homeless shelter called the Mustard Seed and began serving food to the less fortunate. Another project that they came up with was working with teenagers who were struggling to make it in school due to drug addictions, serious home situations and sometimes living on the streets. The project involved bringing attention to these young people's needs through the media. As a result of their work and with the assistance of teachers and myself, the Alberta Safe House Society received some much-needed media coverage and the students received an invaluable education. To reward these young people, the Calgary Police Service allowed me to give the students a day out at the driver training track where they were given a crash course, literally, on being a police officer. One of those young people went on to become Miss Canada. We affectionately called her "cone killer". Supporting our young people and praising them is a part of the peace officer's role.

Suffice it to say, as peace officers our first responsibility is to serve the public through commendation, not through punishment. In Romans 13:4, however, we are called God's servants or ministers to promote good and to do good to those we serve. I will spend a whole chapter looking at the role of the servant.

A Terror to Evil

The next role and purpose we have as law enforcement officers is to be a significant "terror" to those who do evil or wrong. Those who choose to do wrong should experience a varying level of fear depending on the wrong done. As members of the law enforcement community, we bear the authority of our office as well as the tools required to bring the wrongdoer to a place of judgment. For the second time in a very short space, those in law enforcement are called God's servants, this time to bring punishment and not praises. The sword in this verse, literally, refers to the killing instrument, either a knife or sword that was carried by the soldiers of the day. This sword carried the authority of the law as well as the ability to take a life under the appropriate circumstances. In modern times, I believe that sword refers to our uniform which represents our authority as given by the municipal, provincial or federal government. It also refers to the tools of our trade. Because the term ruler refers to all those I've mentioned earlier, the sword refers to the power of the courts to take life, to imprison, restrict freedoms and/or require service to the community or individual to pay restitution for the wrong committed. To those in law enforcement, it includes our firearm, asp, taser or nightstick, pepper spray, hand cuffs, hands and other such tools required to carry out our duties. Clearly, these are times when deadly force is required—where in essence the peace officer must take someone's life because either his life or another's is eminently at risk. God's authority is clear. We are authorized to kill another person by use of a deadly instrument as a servant of God.

Many years ago, during my initial struggle to define who I was as a Christian and police officer, I worked with another young officer. Shortly into our partnership some serious tensions arose for reasons I didn't clearly understand. Finally, I asked this officer what this issue was. He told me he didn't want to work with me in part because I was a Christian and he didn't like that. Finally, he stated that because I was a Christian he was afraid that I wouldn't back him up to the point of killing someone if I needed to. At first I was pretty hurt over his comments but at the same time I understood. There had been other officers who were Christians that had apparently indicated that they wouldn't shoot someone because of their faith.

I believe that this is in part because of a misinterpretation of the commandment of Moses which some interpret as "Thou shalt not kill." (Exodus 20:13) The actual translation from the original Hebrew language is not the word "kill" but "murder." In Matthew 5:21, the King James Version used the words, "Thou shalt not kill." Again, a more careful look at the original Greek language clearly indicates that the words should read, "You should not be a murderer." The word is, again, "murder" not "kill." Chaplain Stephen Lee, in his preamble for the Bible version, *God's Word for Peace Officers*, states "God's Word allows killing in certain instances such as a defense of life, just wars and properly imposed capital punishment."[4] I absolutely agree with this and, as a peace officer, believe that the reference here in Romans gives us God's direct authorization to use a killing instrument as an agent of His judgment when it is absolutely required. I believe this is vitally important to the emotional and psychological well being of police officers who are involved in shootings where they have killed someone. Knowing that the killing of another human being has consent, authority and justification in God's eyes can help in mitigating some of the emotional trauma to the officer. Studies have shown that officer-involved shootings can take a real emotional toll on the officer and cause significant backlash to the officer and his family. I have personally witnessed this occur in several officers that I know and have dealt with. The other important factor is having the same support from the service that employs the officer. The officer himself needs to know two things: 1) the service backs him/her and 2) God backs him/her. Then the healing can begin in earnest. Without these two things, there is a significant likelihood of emotional fallout.

A personal friend of my wife's and mine was involved in a very unfortunate incident where he had to shoot a man of another nationality in a public place after this man had stabbed our friend twice with a knife. This man was running around yelling at people and threatening them. When our friend approached in uniform, the man stabbed him. Our friend jumped back and shot him. Unfortunately, due to political sensitivities our Service did not back our friend quickly due to complaints from this nationality group. The Service did back our friend eventually but the damage had been done and he struggled with disillusionment for the remainder of his career. He continued to be a good cop but was bitter towards the department. It is so important for the officers to feel they have God's approval and the Service's approval.

Romans 13:4 provides the God-given authority to carry out the sometimes awful responsibility of using deadly force. Further to that, those in law enforcement are called the agents of wrath or avengers of God's justice on those who do wrong. There are a few things that need explanation here. As I mentioned previously, this passage refers to all those who are part of a judicial system designed to bring God's laws to the people. At various times in history, the process of that system is minimal and at other times, laborious and drawn out. The point is that those who are part of the system bring God's justice to those who do wrong.

The Avenger of God's Wrath

The word "avenger" or "agent" of God's wrath comes from a Greek word that literally means "the one who carries out justice" or "the one who completes what is right." As law enforcement officers we are to assist in completing what is right, to ensure that justice is carried out. Our duty is to restore peace and righteousness where it was not.

The Scripture says we are agents of God's wrath to execute punishment. There is a great deal of confusion about God's wrath. Most people seem to see God one of two ways. He is either a loving grandfatherly type or a God waiting to zap them whenever they do something wrong. Neither view of God is correct. Again, I'm not a theologian but I do know that Scripture talks a lot about the nature of God. God is, at least, all powerful, all-knowing, ever-present without beginning or end, unchanging, full of grace, mercy, kindness and unconditional love. But Scripture also says that He is a God who hates and experiences wrath. There are two things God is passionate about: people and evil. God passionately loves His people and despite our stubborn refusal to be obedient to Him, sent His son, Jesus, to make a way for us to be in restored relationship with Him. He purchased us back from sin and death giving us His Spirit, a new heart and a new hope for eternal life with Him.

God is also passionate about evil. He is deeply opposed to evil and the sin that comes out of it. The word for wrath means to desire eagerly or earnestly as a state of mind with the purpose of revenge. Revenge goes back to the same word for avenger or agent of wrath. It is the desire to right what is wrong, to restore righteousness. God, according to Scripture, is absolutely passionate about avenging wrong and punishing evil and those who practice evil. Here is what many may miss when they see or read about God's wrath. His wrath is always about restoring people into relationship with Himself. The whole point of the story and life of Jesus was to show us that in and of ourselves we are incapable of being good enough to earn a restored relationship with God. Therefore, because we all have sinned, done things both intentionally and unintentionally that are wrong, we are objects of God's passion against evil. To fulfill the demands of justice and wrath, God placed the requirements of the law on Christ when He sent him—and Jesus willingly went—to the cross to pay the price of our sin. Because payment was made, justice is restored and we can be back into a right relationship with God, through Jesus Christ. Wrong is now righted and relationship restored.

So, as law enforcement officers, our purpose and role is to be agents of God's wrath, to aid in the process of bringing punishment to a person who does evil, so that ultimately they, if they choose, can be restored to a right relationship with God. Our purpose is to restore justice and to be peace makers, righting that which is wrong as a representative of God's love for us.

When I was interviewing officers and spouses across Canada, I was confronted by the reality that there were some who greatly objected to the tone of Romans 13. There was a genuine concern about being agents of wrath. It is described as a "harsh statement." One officer said, "This passage doesn't fit for police officers, maybe soldiers but not "peace makers – Peace Officers"." Another officer said he was not happy with the picture of officers being vengeful. In light of a fuller understanding, I could not agree more with this viewpoint. We, as peace officers, are not to be vengeful for the sake of vengeance. We are to be agents of God's wrath with the intention of bringing people into a restored relationship with the Creator of all laws. That is God's heart and if we are His servants, carrying out the heart and purposes of the Master is the role and function of a good servant.

Sadly, though, there will always be those who pursue evil. They are not interested in right behaviour except for how it will benefit their evil practices. There are people, enemies of God, who will prey on and abuse others. They will take advantage of the weak, naïve, poor and disadvantaged even to the point of murder if it suits their need. You don't have to be a cop long to have seen it in the eyes of some we deal with. Interestingly enough, I have seen it in the eyes of those we would consider model citizens. They are cunning, smart individuals who hide their evil behind so-called good deeds yet their goal is destruction. There are many who will stop at nothing including the murdering of God's servants to accomplish their evil. At the time of writing this book, four RCMP officers, all 32 years and younger, died at the hands of one such person. Many people including the parents of this individual commented on the evil present in this man.

My friend and partner in policing and chaplaincy for many years, Jim Amsing, spent a short time in a small community in Alberta. It didn't take Jim long to learn that there were members of the community who were significant businessmen but who were, in fact, evil. They used their business to hide their illegal activity. They had also gained the support of a local judge who allegedly had a drug addiction. This judge used his position to subvert justice to this community. At one point, a henchmen for one of the businessmen threatened Jim's family. For the first time in his life, Jim had to draw a huge line in the sand. He told the henchman and businessman that he would do whatever it took to stop this harassment and threats. These two got the message but it took extreme action on the part of a peace officer to stop the threats.

Most of us as officers know that when we joined policing we did so out of a genuine desire to serve others and somehow make a difference. We also know that in reality we are in a battle whether we like it or not. Most of the time, we will serve and serve well. Sometimes we will have to fight and fight well. Sometimes we will "fight for what's right as well as peoples' rights," as one female officer said to me. A sergeant I interviewed said, "We are a bridge between heaven and hell. Our job is to keep hell from taking over." In many respects those in the front lines of policing are preventing hell from taking over. In the movie *Saving Private Ryan,* the last scenes focus on a small company of men who are trying to prevent the Nazis from crossing a bridge. The odds are overwhelming and the methods unorthodox because of lack of equipment, but the small band prevails long enough for the reinforcements to arrive and repel the enemy. I realize this is a military example but I believe in many respects this is a picture of the everyday world of policing. We stand at the bridge as law enforcement officers, prevailing until the rest of the judicial system arrives with reinforcements to assist in repelling evil.

We are both the servant and the warrior.

So God has given us our identity, first and foremost, as peace-makers—the very sons and daughters of the Creator. We have infinite value and significance to Him. Secondly, we are called for a purpose, to be servants and warriors. We are called to honour and commend those who do good. We are to be a terror for those who do evil, with the hope of restoring them into right relationships first with others and secondly with God. We are to be warriors who stand against evil in our society, using the tools we have to prevent its advancement, to prevent "hell from taking over."

The role of faith in policing has shown us who we are and why we are here, specific to policing. I would now like to explore how faith impacts our role as servants then as warriors.

Chapter Four
The Role of the Servant

Years ago I began to learn how to study the Bible much the same way as a good detective would study a crime scene and the potential characters involved. I came across a study on the role of the servant. I looked at numerous parts of Scripture that spoke of the servant. In the Old Testament days, three thousand or more years ago, a servant or slave was usually a foreigner brought into captivity through warfare or someone who became a slave as a result of poverty or indebtedness. According to Jewish tradition, a person who was a slave or servant would be under the control of the master, but every seven years the slave was given an opportunity to be free. If however the servant enjoyed working for the master and loved his family, then the slave could choose to remain a slave or servant to the master. If that occurred the master was to permanently mark the servant by driving an awl through the servant's ear, forever marking him or her as willingly serving the master.

In the passage in Romans 13, those who are part of the law enforcement field are called servants of God. We all volunteered, freely and willingly, to come under our master, the public, so we could serve out of a genuine care and concern for the well-being of our community and fellow man. I was listening to a talk show in Calgary about the murder of four RCMP officers when a young man who been accepted to the RCMP Depot Training Center called in. In the face of these men's deaths, this young man couldn't wait to serve his country and people with the same honour and sacrifice these men died with. He was honoured to be accepted to serve people through the RCMP.

As servants of the public, we, like the servants of old, are marked men and women. We willingly accept the badge and uniform, clearly marked out to all whom we serve.

Inspector Jim Sneep of the Toronto Police Service says the uniform "sets us apart," a term referring to what the word "holy" means. He says, "We need to have a healthy attitude to <u>why</u> you wear it, because it is an emblem of people's rights and privileges. It is the greatest symbol of sacrificial public service."

When I joined the Service, I made my oath before God that I would willingly serve the people of Calgary. My service was first of all to God, then the people of Calgary, then the country. It was truly an honour to serve God and His people for twenty five years. I do not regret that service but enjoyed it very much.

Over the past eleven years I have presented to nearly every recruit class that has joined the Calgary Police Service and I've yet to see someone join without a sense of excitement and willingness to serve.

So what constitutes a good servant? I posed the question to police officers and their spouses across Canada. Their responses were remarkably similar. All of these people had been in law enforcement for a minimum of ten years, some beyond twenty-five years of service.

Here is the list of servant characteristics I compiled from their responses: Ethical, moral, standing for right, integrity, giving of self, others first, good listener, objective, compassionate, empathetic, trustworthy, likes and respects people from all walks of life, impartial, effective communicator, honest, loyal, courageous, fair, committed, brave, rectitude, sincere, devoted, honours, righteous, unselfish, fortitude and humility. A law enforcement servant understands that he/she is not God and not the big picture. They have a universal love for mankind. They understand the gift of contribution and bring their skills into the service of others. They are able to stand amid the opposition. They respect the rule of law and are able to make relevant, prudent choices under fire.

This list is fairly comprehensive and when you look at it, overwhelming. Can any one person live up to this list all the time or even some of the time? Yet this is the standard that we set for those who are in law enforcement. How can faith have an impact on this list of qualities and characteristics? Is there some guidance and instruction as to how we carry out our role and purpose in law enforcement? I believe there is a great deal or this book wouldn't get written.

The term in Scripture for servant is the word *Diakonos*, specifically as it relates to those in the field of justice. Diakonos appears to come from two words, one meaning to hasten or pursue, the other meaning to minister, adjust, regulate or bring order to. That sure brings a lot of meaning to those who are police officers, in particular. I can remember more than a few occasions when I hastened very quickly to bring order to a bad situation.

On one occasion, a bar fight had broken out in one of our local western saloons. My partner and I were dispatched along with two other car crews. With lights and sirens blazing, we raced to the scene (we were only blocks away) where we found several people including the bouncers engaged in a whale of a fight. The six of us raced into the scene and ran in to the building to find about a dozen people scrapping. Between the presence of the uniform and some slick maneuvering by us "ministers", we were able to bring order to the bar. Not without losing my snap-on tie and popping most of the buttons on my shirt. I escaped with a few scrapes, but the "ministers" prevailed and several of the drunken combatants were dragged, literally, off to jail to cool down and face a few public mischief charges. I must confess I enjoyed getting there quickly and enjoyed the process of bringing order to the bar. I spoke with the bar staff later on and they really appreciated us showing up. Another client satisfied. Such are the joys of public service.

While I am writing this, my sons and I are working at a cattle ranch. We are voluntarily and willingly working to meet the needs of the ranch manager. We are doing many of the things, like fixing fences and putting up corrals, that he simply doesn't have time to do as he cares for the cows and calves that are coming fast and furious. For me and the boys, it is a lot of fun to see a need and willingly step in to meet that need. That is the role of a diakonos.

Diakonos is also the word given to those who provide leadership and direction in the church. There are similarities of calling and roles given to those in church and community work. If you look at the qualifications for those who minister in the church and those who serve in law enforcement, you see a lot of overlap. Scriptures say a minister should be above reproach, temperate, self controlled, respectable, hospitable, able to teach, not given to drunkenness, gentle, not quarrelsome and must manage his family and household well. It seems to me that these are the people we are looking for in law enforcement.

This leads me to the best example we have of how a servant should live his or her life. One of the best books I've read on servant leadership is *The Servant* by James C. Hunter.[5] It is a parable of a man who goes to a monastery to get some direction in his life. He reluctantly goes but is excited to know that there is a world-renowned business leader who lectures at the monastery. This leader gave up his successful career to pursue a quiet religious life. The book then goes on to describe Jesus Christ as the greatest servant leader ever. Hunter points out that although He could have, Christ did not come from a position of power or might like some other great leaders, but instead from a position of influence from which He gained much authority. He chose willingly to serve others so that His influence became renowned in the regions. His influence was what changed people's lives, not the use of His power to kill and overthrow people and nations. This one man changed the world through a sacrificial desire to serve others for their sake and at the cost, ultimately, of His own life.

As I have already pointed out, police officers need to know their identity, who they are and even whose they are. Secondly, they need to know what their role and purpose is. In both cases, faith helps tremendously in sorting that out. Faith also provides an example of how this is truly lived out in our world.

Christ knew who He was and whose He was. He knew at a very early age that He was the son of God and that He was to be about His Father's business. A very interesting passage is read by Jesus to the leaders of the synagogue, from Isaiah 61:1-2.

> "The Spirit of the sovereign Lord is on me, because the Lord has anointed me to preach good news to the poor. He has sent me to bind up the brokenhearted, to proclaim freedom for the captives and release from darkness for the prisoners, to proclaim the year of the Lord's favor." (NIV)

Here Jesus shows very early in His public ministry that He knew who He was and why He was here. This was very much the servant role that He was to fulfill. What is most interesting to me is that He doesn't finish the quote from Isaiah, which is "and the day of vengeance of our God." The chapters that follow in Isaiah speak of Christ coming to bring the wrath of God to the wicked. The passage of Isaiah shows Jesus as the Servant Warrior but His first role was to come as the Servant.

A second set of verses from Isaiah 42 shows exactly the same pattern. In Matthew's Gospel, Chapter 12:18-21, Matthew quotes from Isaiah 42:1-4 where Jesus comes as the suffering servant. In Isaiah, the verses that follow are very similar to Isaiah 62 where Jesus comes to open the eyes of the blind, free captives from prison and release from the dungeon those who sit in darkness. Again, this is the servant role of Christ first and foremost. What follows in Isaiah 42 is Christ coming as a warrior to triumph over His enemies, specifically those who trust in idols and keep the blind, blind. Again, Christ comes first as the servant but, in the right time, as a warrior to defend the oppressed and defeat evil.

There is a direct correlation between Christ's role and our role in law enforcement. Our first and foremost response as officers is to serve; to find ways, peacefully, to bring resolution and order to difficult situations. We are there to help people see things they had not seen, free people from the bondage they find themselves in and to help release people from their own dungeons where we are able. As was the case with Christ, there are many who refuse to allow that to happen in their own lives but our first response is to help them where we can. We are to willingly hasten to meet a known need for the sake of others. This is our first response.

In this area, when I did my interviews, I was given a word of caution from one I respect greatly. In each and every situation we experience as officers, we should seek to serve first, to seek full understanding of the other's situation from as many sides as is practical, and then try to provide understanding about what can or cannot be done. The caution is this. Often when we are new to our profession there is a sense we are out to save the world or champion for the oppressed. This is often misguided and can lead quickly to a cynical, what's-the-use attitude that becomes detrimental to the officer and eventually his or her family. I frequently see officers taking on various causes only to find themselves worn out, not looking after themselves or their most important relationships, and finally at emotional and psychological risk through harmful addictions. Sgt. Gary Armstrong of the Calgary Police Service Learning Center said that a better word for him is the word *companion*. He felt his purpose as a police officer was no longer to be a champion but a companion. I believe this has solid backing in the life of Christ.

Jesus understood His mission and purpose. He came first to seek and to save the lost through His sacrificial death that paid the penalty of sin, and then to rise to new life giving us the hope of eternal life. This was His cause. There are many including His own followers that wanted to make Him their champion, to push Him to become their ruler and king <u>now</u> so they could be rid of the Roman rule and set up the Kingdom of God here on earth in physical form. That was not Christ's first purpose. He came to be their companion first, to show who God was through His life and example and to serve those God called Him to serve. It is interesting to note that Christ, when He left this earth after His resurrection, sent us the Holy Spirit. The Holy Spirit was to be our comforter, teacher and companion, one who walks alongside of another. So Sgt. Armstrong said our preferred role is that of companion, to come alongside of another human being in the midst of their struggle and walk with them for the period of time we find ourselves involved. We are not to become their champion or we will exhaust ourselves.

Does this mean we are never to champion a cause? No, I don't believe that is true either. What we do need to do is be very sure that we are to bring leadership to a cause and that cause needs to be very selectively chosen. As many others have said, we need to carefully pick our battles. We can't do it all and we were never meant to.

When we as officers are willing to serve people and our community well, we have a greater opportunity to influence change than when we use might and power. There are occasions when we create change in people's lives because we used our power and authority to protect or even rescue a member of the public. It has been my experience and the experience of nearly all that I interviewed that real effective long term change came when we served people well.

Many years ago, I worked in the south end of Calgary where a particular young man was causing a lot of havoc in the community. He had been arrested on numerous occasions for assault, property crimes and robberies. On more than a few occasions I was involved directly or indirectly with this young man. I remember distinctly when my children were very young seeing this person, hair long on one side, shaved bald on the other, walking across the street in front of our vehicle. I told the kids to stay clear of him because he was dangerous.

On a few occasions I would interview "John" (not his real name) and knowing something of his mother's faith in God, I would challenge him about his life. At one time, John and I met again just after he was released from prison. Now he was on a spiritual journey of his own. We spoke again and I tried to encourage him in his journey. Needless to say I was quite surprised about the turnaround. It didn't last however and he committed a series of robberies that landed him back in jail.

A couple of years later, I was returning from a missions trip with some teens when I was floored to see John there picking up one of the adult helpers who accompanied us. As it turned out, John had married the gentleman's sister, a fine Christian woman, and John had turned his life around through his newfound faith. His life is still a struggle but not long after that I had the privilege of doing a preamble for John's testimony as he shared how his life was changed in part because my family had prayed for him and I had treated him with respect (most of the time). In the end it was not by might or power of the law but the service and spirit of God through myself and others that created enough influence for change to occur in this man's life. The power of influence is far greater when people are served even when the rule of law applies.

My chaplain and police partner, Jim Amsing, tells a story of stopping a guy for shoplifting. When the paper work was completed Jim and his partner took this man out for dinner because during his time with this man, Jim had learned about where his life was headed. Jim went to his home to see if the story he was told was true. It was very true and as a result Jim and wife Thelma made meals and visited him at his home. To this day, Jim still has contact and influence in this man's life. It was not because of might or power but because of a willingness to meet the needs of another human being.

One of my favorite passages in Scripture has to do with setting aside might and power so that service and influence can reign. Philippians 2:5-11 says,

> Your attitude should be the same as that of Christ Jesus: Who, being in very nature God, did not consider equality with God something to be grasped, but made Himself nothing, taking the

very nature of a servant, being made in human likeness. And being found in appearance as a man, He humbled Himself and became obedient to death—even death on a cross! Therefore God exalted Him to the highest place and gave Him the name that is above every name, that at the name of Jesus every knee should bow, in heaven and on earth and under the earth, and every tongue confess that Jesus Christ is Lord, to the glory of God the Father. (NIV)

In this passage, the Son of God who had all the glory, power and authority of God and, in fact, was/is God, lays it all aside to take on the role and nature of a servant and becomes a man. He was obedient to the calling on His life to redeem mankind even though it meant His death in the most brutal form known at the time. He humbled Himself. As a result, God exalted Him and because of the influence of His life some day the world will acknowledge who He is and declare him Lord.

As police officers we are bestowed with a significant amount of power to remove freedoms, to arrest, to search and seize property. We train physically to handle the demands of the job. We have equipment that supports the power to use force—deadly force, when necessary. We have a tremendous amount of power and authority. Many times however that power and authority needs to be laid aside so we can do what is best for the sake of others.

I think that this is one of the greatest gifts that the role of faith plays in policing. It has the ability to keep us humble. It has the ability to remind us, as Sgt. Terry Larson said, "We are not God and we are not the big picture." It is a constant reminder that policing, with all its supposed might and power, is ministry more than anything else.

As law enforcement officers we must maintain a spirit of humility. This appears at first to be completely contrary to the image of a macho, "I can handle it myself, thank-you," officer. It is contrary to the culture of policing. Sadly, pride is often the unspoken or sometimes proudly spoken word. In its wake, it has left a lot of broken hurting people at home and in the public. If we serve because we are God's gift to the world, we are in for a terrible shock and a great deal of disappointment. As I mentioned previously, caring about others and putting other's needs first shows up significantly in the character qualities supplied by police and spouses across Canada. Pride was not on the list of anyone I spoke with.

Jesus did what he did in Philippians 2 because of two things: a love for us and a willingness to be obedient to the will of His Father. In *The Serva*nt, James Hunter writes two list, one defining the agreed qualities of a good leader demonstrating authority and leadership, the other defining what love is as described in 1 Corinthians 13.[6] That is best known as the love chapter in the Bible and read or written at nearly every wedding I've seen or been involved with.

Authority and Leadership	*Agape Love*
Honest and Trustworthy	Patience
Good role model	Kindness
Caring	Humility
Committed	Respectfulness
Good Listener	Selflessness
Helped people be accounttable	Forgiveness

Authority and Leadership	*Agape Love*
Treated people with respect	Honesty
Gave people encouragement	Commitment
Positive enthusiastic attitude	
Appreciated people	

When the two lists are lined up—the qualities of a law enforcement officer versus the actions of love—they line up beautifully.

Patience – showing self control

Kindness – giving attention, appreciation and encouragement

Humility – being authentic, without pretences or arrogance

Respectfulness – treating others as important people

Selflessness – meeting the needs of others

Forgiveness – giving up resentment when wronged

Honesty – free from deception, integrity

Commitment – sticking to your choices

Results: Service and sacrifice – setting aside your own wants and needs, seeking the greatest good for others[7]

All of these qualities define a good peace officer and a great servant. In a quote from *The Servant*, Hunter says, "....love, the verb, could be defined as the act or acts of extending yourself for others by identifying and meeting their legitimate needs."[8] That is the role of a diakonos, a servant peace officer.

Chapter Five
The Role of the Warrior

The term warrior in policing can be very controversial. Many officers see themselves very clearly as warriors. Others find the term warrior to be repulsive and not reflective of their roles at all. This became very clear to me as I interviewed officers and their spouses across Canada. Some officers resonated with the role of being at battle with evil—standing in the gap between good and evil and venturing into the realm of evil to penetrate it from within and bring it to its knees. Some relish the thought of taking on evil, facing it square on and slaying the dragon, sword firmly planted in the heart. Behind stands the public cowering yet admiring the courage and fortitude of the warrior.

Others saw themselves not as warriors but as peacemakers who bring peace, calm and control to those who have experienced trauma, suffering and lives out of control. Their role is clearly found in public service rather than in the act of war.

When I used the term warrior there was also a divergence of opinion on what a warrior is. Many saw the term warrior as a violent term used to bring violence to people. It was seen in very negative terms. After all, the Nazis and Hitler were warriors. The African warrior class would bring violence and death to other tribes simply because they were different tribes. Even our Canadian aboriginal populations tell stories of the warrior class going out to make war with other tribes because it was what they did. It was about power, control and violence. It was not about the overall good of humanity but of raising one class of society above all the others to their detriment.

As I write this chapter I am very aware of the diverse opinions among great peace officers as to what our roles are as servant warriors. Therefore, I want to clearly define what I mean when I say we, as peace officers, are also warriors. The role of faith in our role as warriors is equally as important as it is in our roles as servants. God and His word have much to say about a correct view of that warrior, as He does about the servant.

As I mentioned earlier there are interesting passages in the Bible that refer to Jesus Christ first in His role as the suffering servant of God's children yet secondly coming as a warrior meting out justice and destroying utterly those who stand for evil. We are mostly comfortable with seeing Jesus as the servant, laying His life down for the sake of His sheep, yielding His rights as God to become a humble servant. What we often fail to remember is that this was Christ's statement of winning a great war and battle with the evil one. Scripture says that Satan would bruise Jesus' heel but that Jesus would "crush" the head of the enemy. His whole purpose of coming was to save His people by facing the evil one head on and crushing him.

In the Old Testament God Himself is described as a warrior. In Exodus 15, God has successfully routed the Egyptian army when the army chased Israel into the sea and God caused the sea to cover the army and they drowned. God wars and defends His people against the enemy. The Israelites then sing a song, "The Lord is a warrior, the Lord is His name."

In Revelation 19:11, Jesus is seen by the Apostle John as coming on His white horse and with Him come all the saints. He is called faithful and true, the word of God and He comes to judge and to make war. His war is against the evil nations, kings and the evil one.

Throughout the Old Testament, when Israel is called to war, it is almost always under the direct leadership and direction of God. When they do otherwise they were usually soundly defeated. Their wars were often fought in unusual ways because God was fighting for them. Israel defeats Jericho by marching around it seven times, finally blasting their horns and watching the walls of Jericho tumble to the ground. Victory was easy.

In another battle Israel is about to be attacked by a trinity of nations. God tells Israel to watch from a hill while God created such confusion and animosity amongst the nations assembled that they destroy each other, leaving the spoils for Israel simply to pick up. God did the fighting.

Gideon is called upon to fight the Midianites who were constantly harassing and stealing from the Israelites. He pares an army down from 22,000 men to 300. These men fought by crashing pottery and blowing their horns, causing massive confusion for the Midianites who also fight amongst themselves. Israel chases and defeats them handily because God fought for them.

Warring, in God's economy, is just when it has the right cause. In most cases God called Israel to war against a violent and horribly evil nation. These nations often sacrificed their children or their people for the sake of their gods. Or, God defends Israel against attack from others who intended harm and evil to Israel.

In the New Testament, there are many references to the role of the warrior. As mentioned previously, Jesus pays one of His greatest compliments of faith to a man of war, the centurion with the sick servant. The first Gentile Christian was a man of war, a centurion. God chose him because he loved God and His people. One of the first Christians in Philippi was a prison guard. Paul makes numerous references to soldiers, their role, their equipment and their training. He would know; he spent a great deal of time in the presence of them during his imprisonment in Rome.

What is the true role of the warrior? Over and over again in the Bible, the role of God as a warrior was to stand and defend the downtrodden, the oppressed, the poor, the widow and the orphan, and to break the chains of those in prison. He stands in opposition to evil and defends those who cannot defend themselves from evil and the oppressor.

In my research I came across a poem dedicated to those in law enforcement, the armed forces, firefighters, coast guard and emergency medical teams. It was written by Jon Hooper.

"I am a Warrior"

I fight not for glory or fame
For they are momentary
I fight for those who can't
I fight for Justice.
I fight for the oppressed and the down trodden
And if I should lose my life for these just causes, then I have no regrets.
For I serve to protect the innocent
It matters not where or when
For evil knows no boundaries.
Be it fire, flood or the threat of tyranny, I will not Flee
Justice is my weapon
Faith is my Shield

Hope is my armor
Cry not at my passing
For it was my honor to fight for you
Shed not tears of sorrow, but tears of joy,
For now I stand with God.[9]

Hooper is absolutely correct. He stands with God. In Isaiah 58 God points out the wrong of false religion and says true religion does the following:

1. loosens chains of injustice

2. sets the oppressed free

3. provides for the poor

4. shelters the wanderer

5. clothes the naked.

This is the call of the true warrior. In Isaiah 59, God is greatly displeased because He looked and could not find justice. He saw no one upholding justice and He is appalled. There was no one to intervene. So what does He do? His own arm works salvation and His righteousness sustains Him. He puts on righteousness as His breastplate, the helmet of salvation on His head, He puts on the garment of vengeance and wraps Himself in zeal as a cloak. What is His goal? Justice and redemption for His people. If true warriors are to stand with God then justice and reconciliation must be the true purpose of the warrior. The warrior's cause must be that of God's justice only. In Romans 13, the servant of God is also called the agent of God's wrath. The warrior is part of the process that defends the weak and oppressed, the rights of all people to experience justice in its true form and stand in the gap against evil and those who oppress.

A common occurrence among high school students is to have parties with their peers when their parents are not around.

During my time as a school resource officer I became painfully aware of students having parties that were crashed by unwanted peers whose sole purpose was to assault people, and/or steal family property while others distract the students whose house it was. Frequently, I was learning of a number of students getting badly hurt or significant property being stolen. Students knew the perpetrators but were afraid to come forward with the specific information for fear of getting beat up. I gained enough information that I knew who the offenders were but needed people willing to testify. Clearly I desired to prevent this evil and to stand in the gap for the sake of the innocent students but was defeated by the students themselves. Finally, a group of thugs invaded a party where they beat up the student owner of the house so badly that his intestines were twisted. The student nearly died in the hospital. As a result, students came to the forefront and agreed to testify. Enough was enough. I was able to arrest the culprits with the help of members on the street and they were charged and convicted of aggravated assault. As a result of this arrest, we did not have any assaults on students for the remainder of the year. Once we stood in the gap for these students and they felt protected, assaults ceased. Someone stood up for them and they felt more secure.

Paul the apostle speaks clearly of the spiritual armour of God and uses the same metaphors as does Isaiah 59 to describe those who are in the spiritual battle. He describes the armour used by a soldier of the day. A Christian warrior is instructed to put on the full armour of God and to take a stand against the schemes of the devil. Paul warns us, though, that the battle is not against flesh and blood but against the dark forces of this world and the evil forces in the heavenly realms. There is a very real battle going on in both the physical realm and the spiritual realm and we need warriors willing to arm themselves with God's divine power and purpose to do battle with the devil and evil.

Just as God put on the breastplate and helmet so are we to put on the breastplate of righteousness, the belt of truth (integrity) and feet fitted with readiness. We are to take up the shield of faith, the helmet of salvation and the sword of the Spirit, the word of God. And we are to pray.

Can you imagine this kind of peace officer whom God has equipped to do His work, who understands his purpose and is prepared to serve his people? This is a powerful image. This is not the image I was first given, when I was told faith and policing didn't mix. This image is powerful indeed. This is the image of Jon Hooper in his poem. This is an image to be proud of.

Staff Sergeant Chris Butler of the Calgary Police Service gave me an excellent summary of what a warrior is. He reminded me that not all peace officers are warriors. This is a special breed. In his own study of the warrior he identified seven characteristics of a true warrior that are irrespective of all cultures, eras and societies. They are:

Rectitude – when we must die, we must die

Bravery / Courage

Universal Love – benevolence towards mankind

Righteous Action (acting outside of oneself)

Sincerity and Truthfulness

Honour

Devotion and Loyalty

The Belt of Truth

If I compare this list to Paul's list of the equipment of a warrior, there are some definite links. Firstly, the belt of truth is essential to the soldier and warrior because it holds nearly everything else in place. It carries the sword, holds the breastplate in place and enables the soldier to hold his uniform steady so he could move into battle with his legs and feet unrestricted. The belt of truth clearly lines up with sincerity and truthfulness. Without integrity, a law enforcement member will not last or have little value to the people served. If an officer's integrity is in question, in court in particular, his testimony and witness will have little or no effect. Integrity also means being true to oneself and honestly recognizing one's strengths and weaknesses. This requires a significant dose of humility. Virtually all who were interviewed stated that humility is essential.

Unfortunately, many have a very poor understanding of true humility. Let me use a word picture to help. A horse is a very powerful animal and can do harm to its owner if not properly trained. In the days when horses were used in battle, they looked for strong, powerful, fearless horses to ride. A horse was trained to place his power and strength under the direct control of the rider so that when the time came the horse would do the bidding of the rider fearlessly. This is quite something when you consider that horses are prey animals and run at the slightest hint of danger. Under the control of the rider however, the horse will move into danger at the slightest movement and direction of the rider. This is humility. Strength, power and courage, under control.

Humility is essential to integrity because it allows integrity to stand firm in the face of danger while knowing its own weaknesses. True warriors must be men and women of integrity and humility. Butler says, "When the warrior stumbles, he is the first to share his imperfections and struggles with the other warriors that are standing guard with him." The Bible says that a cord of three is extremely hard to break. Warriors who stand together in integrity and sincerity are very difficult to break.

An officer had been involved in shooting an offender who had tried to stab him when the officer tried to arrest him for a serious offence. A few other officers were involved in the incident and were impacted by the event. The offender was not killed fortunately but was significantly injured. As a result of this event, an informal debriefing took place with all of the officers involved in the shooting. During the debriefing, one senior officer shared with a fair bit of emotion the impact the incident had on him. I was particularly impressed because he spoke with humility and sincerity. This freedom of expression opened up the door to a couple of the younger officers to be honest about how they were impacted by this event. These officers stood with each other in integrity and humility and benefitted significantly from each other's experience. This made them stronger officers who were in touch with their humanity.

Breastplate of Righteousness

The second piece of equipment mentioned is the breastplate of righteousness. This compares to the righteous acts and conduct of the warrior. The true warrior always does what is right, regardless of the consequences. In *The Way of the Wild Heart*, John Eldredge says, "Our God is a warrior because there are certain things in life worth fighting for, must be fought for. He makes man a Warrior in His own image because He intends for man to join Him in that battle."[10] The warrior recognizes that there are just and right causes outside of himself that must be fought for. This is why men and women died in our two great wars. Something righteous was being fought for. The breastplate was designed to guard the heart of the righteous just as the bullet proof vest does for the modern day soldier. In the movie *The Cinderella Man*, James Braddock wins a boxing match over a much-hailed contender. After the fight, Braddock is asked why he fights. His response was "milk." He fought because his cause was feeding his family during the Depression and being an example to others. He became an icon of the masses because they stood with him in the cause of feeding their families. A true warrior knows that if he dies, he dies for a righteous cause for the sake of others not himself. "No greater love has any man than to give his life for a brother". This is the call of the warrior.

In Jon Hooper's poem, the warrior fights for justice. In God's economy, if I read Scripture correctly, justice and righteousness are so linked as to be inseparable. You cannot have true justice without those who are willing to act righteously, for the sake of others.

Stu Webber, a soldier himself, wrote *The Spirit Warrior* which affirms the need for a cause bigger than oneself. "This is the common theme in all storied legends of warfare. Most of these stories include long marches....on short notice...over impossible terrain...without food or sleep...to fight overwhelming odds. In these legends, it is the warrior soul, a deeply settled conviction in the rightness of his cause – willpower more than firepower – that propels him in the march and ultimately carries the day.

The warrior soul makes all the difference against long odds. Contrary to the common way of thinking, more than a few students of warfare have recognized that "Right makes might." Half-hearted wars are seldom won. Men fight hardest and longest for a cause that flows out of a just and righteous warrior soul."[11]

Feet Fitted for Readiness

The third piece of equipment is feet fitted for the readiness that comes from the gospel of peace. This is courage and bravery. It is one thing to have a just and righteous cause and the integrity to be true to one's self and others. It is a whole other matter to have feet prepared and ready to move forward into the battle. That requires courage.

I think I need to make a quick statement here, reminding those who are in law enforcement about who the enemy is. The enemy is not necessarily the so-called "scum bag," but rather the evil that is represented. Paul reminds us in this passage that the war is not against flesh and blood, but evil. We must continue to support and assist anyone whose cause is against evil and its oppression and suppression.

Back to courage and bravery. Webster's dictionary says courage is the ability to face danger without fear. Bravery is displaying courage or acting courageously. Quite frankly, I disagree with Webster on the definition of courage. Courage does not act without fear, but in spite of fear.

Sgt. Butler says there is a difference between courage and bravery. I would like to quote his response. Some will not like the full measure of the response but I think it reflects the heart of the warrior, knowing whom the battle is for.

"Is being brave the same thing as being courageous? Not necessarily. Members of search and rescue teams possess bravery that is unsurpassed. They put themselves in positions where death stares them in the face and in fact they are often killed. These brave souls deserve much respect. They represent a very small segment of society that would put their lives at risk time and time again for the sake of a fellow human being. But the warrior's heart burns for the chance to fight evil; to have a righteous battle. To stare death in the face and strike down and destroy the enemy, a warrior enters the arena where the enemy's throat is the only object and the destruction of evil the desire. The warrior does not yearn for this battle out of fear or anger, but only because that is what he is called to do. To have your spirit burn for this battle is courage."[12]

Winston Churchill rightly said, "Courage is the first of all human qualities, because it is the quality that guarantees all others." In his book *Why Courage Matters*, John McAin defines courage as "that rare moment of unity between conscience, fear and action, when something deep within us strikes the flint of love, of honour, of duty. And far from being the absence of fear, courage is having an acute awareness of the danger, seeing fully the fear it produces but having the will to act in spite of it."[13]

As some have said, the warrior's greatest asset is his soul, the passion that burns deep within fueled by the love of mankind and the love of his God. A favorite verse of mine is 2 Timothy 1:7. "For God did not give us a spirit of timidity but a spirit of power, love and of self-discipline."

Coupled with that is 1 John 4:18. "There is no fear in love. But perfect love drives out fear, because fear has to do with punishment. The one who fears is not made perfect in love."

For a peace officer whose feet are ready to move into the battle against evil, a faith that depends on the perfect love of God can bring him to a place where he lives out of a sound, trained mind, a love for his neighbour and a disciplined lifestyle. When he experiences fear—and he will—love drives it out and he acts courageously to do the right thing for the sake of the oppressed, imprisoned and chained, the less fortunate, the poor, those whose rights have been trampled. He faces the evil and finds a way to destroy it.

Shield of Faith

The next piece of equipment for the warrior is the shield of faith. I will equate this to the character of universal love for mankind that Sgt. Butler proposes. The shield was to be used to extinguish the flaming arrows fired by the evil one. The role of the warrior is to love and protect his fellow man from the evils of society that can quickly harm others. Butler says, "A warrior will quickly come to battle to protect any individual, there is no evaluation of worth or status; no thought of risk or gain to self." This is the universal love spoken of.

One image that comes to mind is the image of shield bearers holding the shields in such a fashion so as to create a wall in front of, beside and above themselves from archers firing lit arrows from a great distance. This would allow them to advance forward despite the raining storm of arrows.

During the World Petroleum Congress in Calgary, protestors tried to gain access to cause problems in a few oil company buildings. The Calgary Police Service bike squad used their bikes as shields to prevent access to the building. The bikes created a shield between protestors and the employees inside who were genuinely concerned for their safety. The officers thought nothing of their need to stand and protect these innocent citizens.

Stu Weber describes the shield of faith as a shield designed not specifically for the community. There were two shields used, a small one for personal in-close fighting; the second, which this one refers to, is a longer shield used in community with others.[14]

Hebrews 11:1 defines faith as being sure of what we hope for and certain of what we do not see. Hebrews 11:6 says that without faith, it is impossible to please God because anyone who comes to Him must believe He exists and that He rewards those who earnestly seek Him.

The role of faith in policing is to believe that God exists and that He rewards those who earnestly seek him. It is in many respects the pursuit of love (God is love); a pursuit that will have its own rewards. If we are to pursue God, we are to pursue love. If we are to learn to love God, we must learn to love our fellow man. 1 John 4:20 says, "If anyone says 'I love God,' yet hates his brother, he is a liar. For anyone who does not love his brother, whom he has seen, cannot love God, whom he has not seen."

If faith is at all able to bring us to God, it must also bring us to love, without evaluation of worth or status. Faith is a deep personal trust in God. It is a freeing confidence and abandonment to God, knowing He loves us and cares about our well-being as officers and the well-being of those we shield. As our faith grows, so does our desire and ability to shield others from the evil one and to protect one another and mankind from those bent on harm.

In a recent event, a middle-aged man with a known drinking problem was driving a large truck recklessly towards the city. A completely unsuspecting family was stopped at a red light. The driver of the truck drove into the back of this car crushing the car into half, killing three children and the two adults. The scene was particularly gruesome because it involved children. The police, fire and EMS attended the scene and as warriors had to care for the public who witnessed this but also for the occupants. What was amazing was the desire of the officers, firefighters and paramedics to protect their peers and the public from the difficult scene. They also apprehended the offender and made sure the scene was protected so that this evil could be dealt with properly in court. Later, I witnessed older officers desiring to shield younger officers from the emotional toll. I saw nearly all deal with the anger towards the evil that had been done and an ache over the fact that they could do nothing to help the family who died. This is the shield of faith.

All of us in law enforcement carry a badge which symbolizes the shield. That badge says we are sworn to protect and serve, to shield people from injustice. The shield of faith means we carry God's badge to shield His people from injustice as a representative of His love and compassion for His people. Inspector Jim Sneep of Toronto Police Service says that the shield or badge "is an emblem of people's rights and privileges and is the greatest symbol of sacrificial public service. It is not a symbol of power or authority." The shield of faith is designed to protect rights and privileges as an expression of universal love!

Helmet of Salvation

The helmet of salvation is next. I have equated this to the character quality of rectitude, of being in a right relationship or conduct. The concept of salvation means to be saved from being in a wrong relationship and placed into a correct relationship with self and others and in particular with God. It means to be delivered from danger, spiritual and eternal.

For Sgt. Butler, rectitude meant the ability to deal well with death if it was necessary, because of right actions and right relationships. If you recall, Bruce Siddel wrote about the role of faith in preparing a person to deal with death. Better to have processed salvation for eternal reasons so one can better deal with the threat in front of you.

A helmet is designed to protect the head against blows to it and allow the warrior to stay focused on the task. He will be able to think clearly, discuss right conduct and attitude, and perform what is necessary effectively. If you get your "bell rung," clear thinking goes out the window. If your soul is in the right relationship with the Creator, death becomes less of an issue and if you must die as a result of the right actions, your soul rests in the salvation provided by the Creator. Death no longer holds its permanence but is a transition into the presence of a loving Creator. As Butler says, "There is no fear of death; it does not hold the warrior ransom. The samurai call this *mujobodai shin*, which means the wisdom of impermanence. From God's perspective, salvation removes us and delivers us from being permanently separated from God to a place where we are permanently present with God regardless of our physical body's condition."

The helmet of salvation, according to Stu Weber, is intended to protect us from "disorientation, doubt and discouragement."[15] Sometimes when practicing rectitude, it is difficult because often there is a feeling of being alone in the struggle to do the right thing when many are tempted or are not doing the right thing. It's been said, "For evil to flourish all it needs is for good men to do nothing." For many officers, this statement seems to be true. Evil has its way because we watch good men do nothing. It can be a lonely, discouraging place. The helmet of salvation can help prevent doubt and discouragement when we see the results of the evil one's attacks. Faith in the salvation provided can encourage us to stay focused on the task at hand without a fear of death and with the wisdom of impermanence.

The helmet is designed to protect the head and metaphorically from bad thinking or some call it "stinking thinking". This is where the lies we tell ourselves far too often and the arrows of doubt the enemy fires our way about our ability as an officer can cause serious injury to maintaining a positive attitude and keeping things in focus on what God says our role and function is. Cynicism within policing as mentioned is a significant character problem that creeps in for most officers who have forgotten their rightful place in society and God's economy. Cynicism crawls in when we lose our ability to see ourselves making a difference in this broken world and doing what's right when all others seem to refuse. The helmet of salvation can protect against such poor thinking common to many of us. God is in us, working out His salvation for His people through our efforts to restore and protect. We just don't always get the pleasure of seeing the difference made, yet we must carrying on believing that what we are doing for good and right is making a difference.

It was this kind of reprogramming that I needed to undergo when I had my own breakdown spoken of in my own story. I had a bad case of "stinkin' thinkin'" and needed to put my mind back into its protective covering of God's love and salvation for me. When I was able to identify the lies of the enemy and of myself as a direct blow to my head (thinking), I was better able to understand my role as a police officer and ultimately a chaplain. I haven't always gotten it right even still but I understand the process better and usually recover quicker.

Sword of the Spirit

The sword of the Spirit is the last piece of equipment Paul mentions in the armour for the believer. The sword refers to the Word of God. Hebrews 4:12 says, "The Word of God is living and active. Sharper than any double-edged sword, it penetrates even to dividing soul and spirit, joints and marrow; it judges the thoughts and attitude of the heart." Jesus said, "Man does not live by bread alone but by every word that proceeds from the mouth of God." The Word of God tells us how we are to live, who God is, what He has done for us and leads us to the person of Jesus Christ. We define our values, our lives by this Word. Much of our North American history, laws and values were defined by the Word of God.

Sgt. Butler suggests that the character quality associated with the warrior is loyalty and devotion. "Devotion to one's values first, above all things; for the corruption of a man always begins with a betrayal of his values." Devotion and loyalty to one's values are paramount to being a successful warrior. The Word of God then provides us with our values and as warriors we need to be devoted and loyal to the Word of God, the sword of the Spirit to give us moral guidelines on how to do our jobs.

Police services all over the country have value statements that are supposed to be the guiding principles under which they choose to operate. From these guiding principles come their policy statements which give direction to peace officers on how they are to conduct their business from completing check-up slips to chase procedures.

For example, when I asked Sgt. Terry Larson what qualities make a good peace officer, he went directly to the core values of the Calgary Police Service. Why? Because these qualities represented all that was good, right from the sword of the Spirit that defined how a good officer should conduct himself. Those values are honesty, integrity, ethics, respect, fairness, compassion, courage and commitment. How these values are lived out and our loyalty to these values can be found in God's Word.

Another aspect of policing that relates to the values by which we conduct ourselves when compared to the sword of the Spirit, God's Word, is how it relates to our weapons. For the soldier Paul was comparing to a follower of Jesus, the sword was their weapon of offence and defense. To the modern-day warrior, the handgun or tools on our belt refer to the equivalent weapon. As warriors we must be competent in the use of our weapons. For most of us, a great deal of time is spent training and honing our skills with our weapons. Many hours are spent practicing our shooting skills so if the time comes, God forbid, that we have to shoot, we will be able to do what is required effectively and accurately.

In the movie *The Last Samurai*, Tom Cruise's character spent hours upon hours, days upon days, perfecting his ability both to defend himself with his sword but also to attack. It put him in a good position when the time came to use his skills as a warrior. Other movies show characters that use great skill to show would-be thugs that messing with them would be a painful experience only to have the thugs run in another direction.

Several years ago, the Calgary Police Service had a computer program that was similar to an upscale video game. I was able to "practice" on this game. In the scenario I was given, I was forced to shoot a bad guy who pulled a gun out at me from behind a truck. I am most proud to say that I dispatched this would-be assailant in three-quarters of a second from holster to a shot centre mass with my first round. The next two rounds missed but that didn't matter to me. It showed me that all the training and practicing I'd done would pay off if faced with a "have-to-shoot" real life drama. To the day I retired from policing I would practice drawing my gun quickly from many different positions so I knew I could move quickly if I had to. This gave me great confidence to believe that if things went bad quickly, I had a greater chance of survival because I was prepared.

I don't believe it is any different when it comes to the sword of the Spirit. As officers of faith and purpose as given by God, if we are skilled in the use of God's Word our ability as warriors and peace makers will be significantly improved. James 3:17-18 says, "But the wisdom that comes from heaven is first of all pure; then peace-loving, considerate, submissive, full of mercy and good fruit, impartial and sincere. Peacemakers who sow in peace rain a harvest of righteousness." (NIV)

This sounds an awful lot like the values that an officer needs to be devoted and loyal to do the job most effectively. As peace officers called of God, we need to know God's Word and the voice of His Spirit. Many false things have been said and done in the name of God and His Word that have been hurtful and destructive to many people. I am reminded of the story of Jesus being tempted in the desert by the devil. A couple of times the devil uses the words of the Old Testament to claim authority or show God's protection in order to tempt Jesus to submit in some way to the devil's desires. In all cases, the devil misrepresents the Word of God but Jesus, knowing the intent and purposes of God, used the Word of God to defeat the enemy. Just as a warrior knows his weapon well, so a peace officer needs to know God's Word well so that peace can be sown in a bad situation and the harvest of righteousness can be seen.

The heavenly wisdom of God's Word can and will provide the warrior of faith with the necessary skills to adhere to the values God has called us to in the battle against evil as His servant warrior.

The role of the warrior for a police officer is an important role when kept in the context of God's calling to those in law enforcement. It is one component in the greater view of the justice that God has laid out for government. The warrior is never to act out of independence but rather in submission to a higher power, whether that is the supervisor, police service, government or God. Humility remains a significant component of the warrior.

The role of the warrior is to protect the innocent and the down-trodden against evil, and to stamp out evil where it can be found. It is to be an instrument of God's love, mercy and justice. To do any more is to step outside the bounds of God's authority and will oftentimes create damage and destruction in its stead. We are called to be warriors courageously taking on evil but this must always be balanced with our roles as servants to the public because we are indeed the sons and daughters of God.

Chapter Six
Leadership as a Servant Warrior

A vitally important role in law enforcement is the area of leadership and how it impacts the law enforcement officer. Few areas can have as great an effect on the morale of officers as leadership. With poor leadership comes poor morale and with poor morale comes poor service to the public. Although I was never promoted I sat under the leadership of many good leaders and know first hand how leadership or lack thereof affects the ability of an officer and team to perform their duties and continue to be motivated to do those duties.

Another area where the role of faith has a place is in great leadership. If we are able to put our faith in a leader who has his faith in God, then we can be sure of doing God's work even better; not perfectly but better. As mentioned in my story, the Calgary Police Service leadership that knew me in my earliest years made a wise choice to put me under the authority of a leader whose faith was firmly placed in Jesus. He was able to motivate, mentor and guide me as I learned the ropes of policing while struggling with being a person of faith in an environment that discouraged and challenged faith at every turn. Sgt. Barry Davis introduced me to other police officers who were also people of faith so I could feel that I didn't walk alone. He cared about me as an individual and put me with people who could teach me and encourage me when I was discouraged. He, for me, was a good leader. He seemed to care more about principles and values than policy and procedure, although they are all important.

In recent years, certainly in the policing community that I am familiar with, there has been a large movement to having policy for virtually every aspect of policing. One area where this is particularly true in Alberta and elsewhere is in the area of chases. So much so that chases have become, essentially, a thing of the past. Some of this is very good because lives may be saved as a result. Unfortunately it has become an area where officers are more likely to get negative feedback than anywhere else. It has become so policy-driven that it is virtually impossible to engage in a pursuit of a bad guy without breaching some policy and ultimately getting your knuckles rapped. This then can lead to an inability to get promoted or seek a new position because of the negative paperwork. In a recent chat with a police leader, it was noted that because officers are quite smart, they have found ways around policy. So what happens? Policies get rewritten to cover the new findings.

I had a conversation with a deputy chief several years ago reflecting on what policy does for people. His position, rightfully so, is that policy is to be a guideline for officers in carrying out their duties. It is to give direction to how service to the public is to be given. It is also necessary for the Service to show it has done its part to protect itself from liability. Much of this is driven, of course, by lawsuits.

We are now in a time when civil lawsuits are driving much of policy generation. Police services are quick to jump at establishing policy so that they are covered legally. The problem is, it often hangs the officer out to dry. It has truly gotten to the point where policy manuals are so thick that it is virtually impossible for any one police officer to live up to the standard that policy now requires.

What is even more interesting is that lawyers are now using those same policy manuals as weapons to sue law enforcement agencies because they didn't adhere to their own policy. In a recent discussion with a corporate lawyer, several examples were given where agencies were being successfully sued for this very reason. In my discussion with the deputy chief, I said a very similar thing. While policy is supposed to be great as a guideline, it has now become an instrument to punish people. It has become a weapon that demoralizes officers into feeling that they can hardly carry out their duties without breaching some policy.

What has all this got to do with good leadership and the role of faith in policing?

This very thing was occurring thousands of years ago. God had set out a guideline and direction for living that was to guide His people into right living. This right living would bring them great blessing. Trouble is, they could not or simply refused to live by this standard. Secondly, a group of people, Pharisees and religious leaders, rose up to give even more policy as to how people were to live, rules the Pharisees themselves could not live up to.

In and of themselves, the rules and guidelines set out by God and formed by man were not wrong. In fact, the Ten Commandments are a holy set of rules that if lived by *would,* in fact, have given great blessing to the people. The law was good and righteous but people could not live up to the standard and found themselves judged. Then Jesus comes along and preaches one of His greatest sermons known as the Sermon on the Mount. The standard He sets in this message is even higher, making it even more impossible to achieve, proving that all of us fall short of the standard God has established. That was His point, though, to show that none of us can live up to this place of perfection. This is why He came. Because He did live up to this place of perfection, He became the righteous sacrifice needed to pay the consequences for our failure to live up to policy. He became the payment for our civil judgment because we couldn't live up to the demands.

Jesus then set another standard and reminded the people of God's greatest standard. He reduced the laws to principles of practice and values that by His help we could live up to. He said the greatest commandments were: 1) to love God with all your heart, soul, mind and strength, and 2) to love your neighbour as yourself.

All the laws and policies were accomplished in these two laws, period!

I think Jesus' point is this: all the laws of God are good but we can't live up to them. He died to pay the price of our inability to live up to them. So, by faith, we are to trust Jesus with our lives and live according to the principles and values He has established for which the burden is far less and through His help we are able to do.

The implications to policing are profound. Truth is that policy isn't wrong; in fact, it is probably very right. But no one can live up to the full requirements. Therefore we need to live rather by principles and values shown clearly by leaders within policing.

In my research with police and spouses across Canada, no one said that good leadership held intently to policy, enforcing policy on those they lead. All spoke of great principles of leadership that encouraged and motivated those that followed their leadership.

In Wheaton, Illinois, Police Chief Mark Field has taken a very bold step in the policing field. He has virtually thrown out his policy manual and has begun a significant principle-based campaign to clearly and understandably set values before his officers that guide their behaviour.

In a two-part article set out in *The Ethic Role Call*, Summer & Fall 2001, Field has this to say:

"This is not an anti-management treatise. We are not suggesting rule books should be thrown out the window. Instead, we want to redirect "punitive rule making" and substitute "rule guiding." Every organization must set expectations and ground rules and when officers behave otherwise, corrective action must be undertaken immediately. But rules, when taken to extreme, can be counterproductive and destructive to morale and performance."[16] Amen.

In Part Two of his article, he goes on to say, "Instead, leaders must develop and maintain policies and procedures that maximize the improvement of those who perform the complex job of law enforcement. Training must emphasize the link between principles and tasks and employees must be clear on the principles that apply to their specific jobs; especially those high risk/low frequency events."[17]

For leaders to make a difference the focus must be on principles. Just like the old adage for parents, far too often we major in the minors and minor in the majors. We need to major on the majors not the minors.

Much of Paul's letter to the Romans in the Bible focuses on the role that the law played. The law was good and perfect; unfortunately no one could live up to the demands of the law. All of us would fall short of the expectations. Therefore we need to focus rather on faith and the finished work of Christ and then attend to the most important things.

I would like now to address those most important things from the view of one of the centurions Jesus mentioned in Luke

7. Much has been written about Jesus' leadership but I'd like to take it from this law enforcement officer's perspective. Included will be an overview of characteristics gleaned from officers and spouses across Canada.

Luke 7:1-10

When Jesus had finished saying all this in the hearing of the people, he entered Capernaum. There a centurion's servant, whom his master valued highly, was sick and about to die. The centurion heard of Jesus and sent some elders of the Jews to him, asking him to come and heal his servant. When they came to Jesus, they pleaded earnestly with him, "This man deserves to have you do this, because he loves our nation and has built our synagogue."

So Jesus went with them. He was not far from the house when the centurion sent friends to say to him: "Lord, don't trouble yourself, for I do not deserve to have you come under my roof. That is why I did not even consider myself worthy to come to you. But say the word, and my servant will be healed. For I myself am a man under authority, with soldiers under me. I tell this one, 'Go,' and he goes; and that one, 'Come,' and he comes. I say to my servant, 'Do this,' and he does it." (NIV)

When Jesus heard this, he was amazed at him, and turning to the crowd following him, he said, "I tell you, I have not found such great faith even in Israel." Then the men who had been sent returned to the house and found the servant well. Luke 7:1-10

Here are the principles of leadership that I see from this centurion:

1. Value people.

2. Seek to do the right thing.

3. Have the support and respect of others.

4. Take action.

5. Understand authority and humility.

6. Has view to the big picture.

If we practice these principles we won't live by policies that kill, rather we will have life-giving results.

Principle 1. Value People

The centurion valued his servant and those who worked for him and under him. He sought help for someone who was well below his social status. In interviews across the country, the number one principle of leadership was caring for people you serve, both on and off the job. This is very reflective of the servant leadership spoken of earlier. The consensus is that we want leaders who care for people, help others succeed without being authoritative and are committed to people over the organization. When I was seeking promotion I worked for a leader who cared a great deal about me. He gave me his time and energy to help me look as good as possible before those in charge of the promotional process. He truly served me. As a result, he had my support and respect and I was willing to make him look good as well.

A good leader sees the potential in others and encourages them forward. Sometimes this is done with those who have made significant mistakes but because a good leader saw potential and didn't give up on that person, that person grew into a strong police officer. This is what one sergeant I had did for me. He mentored me through some of my young and immature mistakes and encouraged me forward. This leader was a man of faith and he valued people.

Another characteristic of good leaders who value people is remembering where they came from and the roles of those under their leadership. One leader, a duty inspector now retired, was just such a man. Though not a man of specific faith, he never forgot where he came from or the role of those under him. Frequently he was seen working shoulder to shoulder with his men and women. He was respected and loved because of it.

A few years ago, the Calgary Flames did very well in the playoffs going to the Stanley Cup finals. My partner and I were working the Red Mile, a local downtown street with numerous drinking establishments turned into an eight-block party. I got a headache for some reason—probably all the noise. We were working with the Chief of Calgary EMS who had taken a post on the same corner. I asked if he had some Tylenol. He looked through his kit and didn't. The next thing I know, he disappears for several minutes and comes back holding a small bottle of Advil he'd purchased with his own money and gives me the bottle. A small thing maybe, but I respect to this day that act of service to me and it increased my respect for him even more. This man too is a man of faith.

Principle 2. Seek to do the right thing.

The centurion saw his sick servant and sought to do the right thing. He heard about Jesus and sent a delegation to check out the truth of the matter. Getting the facts and seeking the truth before taking specific action is vitally important to making and taking informed action.

One of the things that frustrated me as a young officer was the unwillingness of many officers to explore the truth of something, in particular, the Christian faith. These people were trained investigators but they wouldn't explore or investigate the truth of the Bible. Their standard answer was "Well, that's your interpretation." The centurion had a need, heard about Jesus, investigated the claims then took action to benefit his servant.

Several points come from doing the right thing. In the survey, honest integrity, wisdom, fairness and impartiality, consistency and predictability all rank right under valuing people as the next most important characteristics of leadership. All of these things fall under the principle of doing the right thing regardless of the circumstances or who is asking. It is always righteous behaviour that gains the greatest respect from those being lead. This refers back to the breast plate of righteousness that a warrior wears to protect his heart and life.

Staff Sgt. Steve Lorne is a friend whom I served many years ago as his officer coach. Steve is a man of faith. In recent years, he'd been working toward his Staff Sergeant ranking. He had completed all his requirements and thought that he'd completed the fitness component required to get the promotion. Previously some others had been promoted despite inadvertently missing the fitness component. This created quite a stir that was undermined by upper management. Steve learned that he did not have the fitness part done and went in and removed himself from the list. He had worked very hard for the promotion and could have tried to get through but because of his faith and desire to honour God, he withdrew his application. The next year, he made sure he had done the work and was promoted. Integrity benefited him and he gained the respect of his peers and leaders.

Principle 3. Support and Respect of Others.

In Luke 7, the centurion had received the honour and respect of the people he served and had an excellent reputation. A good reputation is required to be a strong leader. It is this reputation that causes people to actually desire to follow that leader. The Jewish people came to Jesus and asked for His help because this centurion had assisted building the temple and loved the people of Israel.

For many years, the Calgary Police Service Homicide Unit was lead by a very reputable Staff Sergeant. He had a very high expectation of his men and women because it was a very demanding, high profile unit. He was creative and used his wisdom many times to lure the main suspects into providing enough evidence to obtain convictions. At one time, the homicide unit had an extremely high rate of clearance on homicides. His men and women wanted to stay with his unit because of his reputation.

He had many a struggle with management because he cared for and fought for his men and women. He was loved and respected because of this. He had high expectations but served his people very well.

In Scripture, the role of a deacon is a leadership role and comes from the same root word in Greek as the term used for those in law enforcement, *diakonos*. There are specific instructions given as to the qualifications of this leader in the church. One of those is having a good reputation with outsiders. 1 Timothy 3:7 says, "He must have a good reputation with outsiders so that he will not fall into disgrace and into the devil's trap."

It is a good reputation that helps prevent the officer from falling into a trap and falling into disgrace. When you have a good reputation, there is a strong desire to keep that reputation and it acts as a deterrent from getting yourself into greater trouble, particularly in the presence of those you lead. Sadly, I've seen and heard of far too many leaders who have fallen from grace because of an impropriety that ruined a reputation. Many times however the poor reputation was already there.

I recall several times in my street duties where a one night stand with a lovely bar patron was very much a possibility. In part because of my reputation as a Christian officer, I was able to resist any such temptation because I feared losing the respect of my family and my peers.

One indiscretion for a police leader can lead to a poor reputation for many years and it can impact a career for a long time. Unfortunately, people don't tend to forget. Better to find or be a leader of a good reputation. It will protect him and the Service from certain embarrassment.

Principle 4: Take Action

The fourth characteristic of the centurion in this story was that he took action. He did not wait around in hopes that Jesus would come by his place or town so he could look after his servant. He cared, sent ambassadors, checked out what needed to be done and asked for the help he needed from an outside source for the sake of one he cared for. As a soldier, he understood the importance of making a decision based on the best information possible and then taking the required action.

In the survey I conducted, taking action was rated very high among the officers. The ability to take charge of a situation was essential for good policing to take place. One of the officers I spoke with really appreciated one of his leaders because he was "audacious and innovative." In the movie *The Guardian*, Kevin Costner plays a rescue swimmer who due to a traumatic event is asked to teach at the Coast Guard academy. He is audacious and innovative in his style of teaching and leading these young men and women. At first, his style is not appreciated by those in charge but his great reputation with others and his obvious results produced a strong, capable team of rescue swimmers. Sure, this is Hollywood, but this kind of leadership is truly respected by those who must follow.

Strong leaders take action for the cause of those they lead. As mentioned one of the best leaders I had took action for me for the benefit of my career. That same leader took action on behalf of another officer many years later when this man's infant daughter became gravely ill. He took a stand for this officer and saw to it that he was able to look after his sick daughter and to a lesser degree unwell wife without having the burden of losing his income to do so. This was great leadership for the cause of another that earned the respect of those around.

A third take-action principle is to get involved with those you lead. It is one thing to direct your men; it is another to get involved with them in the battle. I mentioned a couple of leaders who were loved because they got involved with the battle. Another friend, Inspector Bill Webb, led well because of his example and his involvement with his men. During the G-8 Summit training that occurred in 2001, many days went into preparation of our Public Order Unit. One of the drills in training was to walk through flames and maintain composure should rioters throw incendiary devices. Their equipment was designed to protect but Insp. Webb led the charge and physically showed his men that they would be okay. He could have told someone else to do it but rather he led the way and gained the confidence of those he would lead. He walked the talk.

Principle 5. Understands authority and humility

This principle is the most crucial principle in the story of Jesus and the centurion. The centurion showed his complete understanding of the role authority takes in all our lives, and how humility plays into authority. The centurion knew that he himself was under authority, that he had authority over his men and attached to that there was an expectation of submission to that authority. Submission requires a level of humility, that great power under control and submission of its master. It is humility that allows authority to have its place. Much of Romans 13, which I spoke of earlier, talks about the role submission to authority requires. The centurion submitted to the authority of Jesus because he believed in Jesus' power, authority and ability to do what he asked of Him. There was an implicit trust in the One to whom he submitted himself. Ultimately it was trust in God to heal his servant. This is what Jesus responded to with amazement and prompted the greatest compliment that came from Jesus' mouth to another human. No greater faith had been seen in all Judea.

The Bible tells us that all authority is given by God so when we live in humble submission to those in authority over us we are actually submitting to the authority God has placed over us. There is a defined limit to that authority however as no man should submit to ungodly edicts. This leads to Hitler and other mass murderers including the likes of David Koresh. God will deal with these evil men in His time. Yet even great evil God somehow uses for good. As a result of the great wars, a great evil (Hitler) was extinguished and a new Jewish state arose which in and of itself was told of many centuries ago in prophetic literature. Whether you agree with it or not, sympathy for the Jewish people as a result of their slaughter as a people group created such sympathy towards the Jews that the United Nations was willing to risk giving them a recognized state which sadly has created huge social, moral and ethical struggles in the Middle East. Whether seen as good or bad, this is what seems to have been predicted thousands of years ago for Israel. God has His purposes beyond ours and we are invited to submit to His purposes.

God is in control ultimately and under normal circumstances our submission to those in authority qualifies us to be leaders of others because we have learned submission to authority and to God Himself.

In our survey of members and spouses, the willingness to balance personal involvement against the role of authority was noted several times. Knowing that one is in a position of authority can often go to people's heads and they don't balance personal relationships with others well. The ability to balance this important aspect of leadership goes a long way in gaining the respect of those who follow as seen by those who served the centurion. This kind of leadership shows accountability and mercy at the same time. Discipline rather than punishment is the motivation for this type of leader.

The most important principle of leadership that rises from understanding authority and humility is servant leadership. This ranks second only to caring for people in the interviews conducted. This is upside-down leadership compared to the way most of the world seems to operate.

James C. Hunter, in his book on servant leadership *The Servant*, uses a diagram that shows how this style of leadership is upside-down. The model looks like this:

Leadership
Authority
Service/Sacrifice
Love
Will[18]

Essentially servant leadership begins with the choice of the human will to act according to the verb love. I spoke of this earlier. Love cares for people and acts in service and sacrifice for the benefit of those being led. These acts of service and sacrifice lead to a level of authority that is gained more through influence than position. This authority allows a person to give leadership because people are willing to follow. Trust has been gained and people are willing to submit humbly to this style of leadership. This is the very model Jesus Himself gave us. It is the model I have witnessed operate most effectively. These are the principles of leadership that give rise to innovation and life. Leading by rules and positional power leads to death of morale and stifles ingenuity and creativity. Understanding authority and humility is essential to servant leadership.

Principle 6. Keeps the Big Picture in Mind.

It is clear from the story of the centurion that he understood the bigger picture. He was a man who understood the bigger needs of the people he served. He was able to see the results of building a temple for the Jewish people and caring for this people. As a result, in the details of life he cared for the individuals and saw their needs met.

There is little doubt that leadership requires vision. There is a determining of the big picture and sticking to it. However, people will not respond well if it is apparent that there are political motivations. Several people commented that political agendas on the part of their leaders did not go over well with them. They found it quite difficult to follow this kind of leader. The vision was not big enough and often self-serving.

True vision can inspire and create a passion in others to accomplish something that has lasting, far-reaching effects. Several years ago, an Inspector I had the privilege of working with had a vision for a funeral policy that would be the finest in Canada and provide an honour to both our serving members and our retired members. This policy would include all civilians as well. He gathered a team to himself including a second inspector who also had a passion for our members and employees being honoured. This vision was unfortunately borne out of necessity due to a significant number of young officers being killed either on duty or going to and from duty. Inspector Brookwell clearly laid out the goals, assigned and trusted people with the tasks and expected to see the results. He also cared about the people more than the policy. Although he was not a religious person, he understood the important role faith played at this kind of time for the officers involved and also for their families. Cst. Jim Amsing and myself were included in the plan. This planning and vision resulted in the most comprehensive funeral directive seen in Canada and is now being sought after by other police services. It includes a whole array of services offered to the families, a new funeral coach used to transport the deceased member or employee with CPS cresting and a good relationship with several funeral homes in Calgary now familiar with how we honour the dead. Our police families have expressed their deep appreciation for how their loved ones were honoured and said the healing process was lightened because of the honour given. This required a vision without political agenda, large enough to benefit many and gain the passion of those who followed the lead.

The Bible says that "without a vision, the people perish." They are lost and have no direction. A leader who is able to instill vision, has the respect of others, pursues the right thing and chooses to serve the people will have those who will follow to accomplish a God-given task.

Vision requires that the goals set are accomplishable. It must adhere to the values of the service involved. Vision also requires risk. Failure may result but only as part of the learning curve to success.

Those who choose to lead need to have a clearly defined vision that can be communicated effectively. This is the call of the servant warrior leader.

The servant warrior leader follows the example of the centurion Jesus honoured. They will

Value people

Seek to do the right thing

Have the support and respect of others

Take action

Understand authority and humility

And have a big-picture vision.

Chapter Seven
The Care and Training of the Servant Warrior

The care and training of a servant warrior is an interesting thing. In my experience, most peace officers absolutely love the training aspect of being a peace officer. When we had an active training day, I couldn't wait to get out in the field, out of the classroom for the fun part. I loved driver training, flying around the track as fast as or faster than I dared, tires screaming, engine roaring and brakes smoking. Is there any other way to do it? I love this part of being a Diakonos – remember...one who hastens to bring order from chaos for another. I particularly liked the hasten part.

Although created out of the tragic events of Columbine in Colorado and Taber in Alberta, the rapid response training we did to prepare for a shooter in schools or businesses was a blast. It was like real life paintball, using our own weapons with special rounds that had paint rather than lead. It was fun-and-games for sure. We all thoroughly enjoyed that. Hearts were pounding and the pressure was on, because you had to protect your team but also take out the shooter (usually a personal friend that we took great pleasure in shooting at and causing pain too....sadistic lot).

It was never much of a problem to stimulate officers to do the training part. It was the caring for part that was a concern to me. I remember when I joined the job, many officers were in poor shape physically, drank more than they should and often had very difficult personal lives through divorce or breakups, and in and out of numerous relationships. Their personal lives were not healthy. Sleep habits were always difficult and continue to be due to shift work, court, overtime and the steady demands of the job. Looking after yourself was a difficult process. Looking after your family, was even more so. Over the years I have seen an improvement in the physical fitness of our members with better training facilities in all the offices, less drinking as a social habit and a greater desire, it seems, to spend time with family and friends. All of this is good but an improvement is still needed.

I believe a human being is made up of three components: the mind, the body and the spirit. As peace officers and servant warriors of God and the public, we have a responsibility to care for ourselves and our families, and to train effectively for the difficult task we have to do. This is the focus of this chapter. What direction do we have from our faith that can guide our thinking, feeling, physical bodies and spiritual lives so we can serve people well and fight victoriously over evil? Once again I believe there is significant guidance for our lives through our faith in a God who cares about who we are and what we do.

1. The Mind

The human mind is an amazing thing, controlling and completing thousands of tasks a minute, many of them done without even thinking about it. It accesses, stores and retrieves millions of bits of information every second. Yet many researchers say we are using only a small percentage of our brain's capacity. Awesome! Truly a marvelous gift from the Creator for his creation.

For my purposes I would like to look at the mind from three characteristics: the will, the emotions and the mind, specifically knowledge and wisdom. I believe that the Bible frequently references the heart to describe the mind, the will and the emotions. It is the heart of a man that God appeals to and Scripture teaches. I believe it is the heart of the man that guides him into either good or evil. That is why it is vitally important that a true servant warrior look after his mind. It is the throne room of his life.

A couple of places in scripture speak to the importance of the mind. Romans 8:6 says, "The mind of the sinful man is death, but the mind controlled by the spirit is life and peace." If we allow our minds to be controlled by the baser side of our humanness, we will experience death in many forms. This is what I see regularly with peace officers whose minds are distracted by the cynicism of policing. This is the stuff that Kevin Gilmartin speaks about in his book, *Emotional Survival for Law Enforcement.* The cynicism of the mind focused on the negative side of policing kills the heart of the officer, minimizing his ability to love well at home or even at work where he finds his greatest satisfaction. Little will fully satisfy unless the mind is focused on the things that bring life.

Recently, I was talking with a friend who was traveling down the highway and had to swerve to avoid hitting a deer carcass on the road. Birds were pecking at the carcass. At that moment he was reminded that from time to time he too pecks at the things that are dead. It was an interesting moment of introspection. It is easy to get caught up in the things that are dead – sometimes too easy – rather than concentrate on the living things of the mind.

Another favorite verse of mine is 2 Timothy 1:7. "For God has not given us a spirit of fear, but of power and of love and of a sound mind." This is truly a verse for the servant warrior. Fear is a part of the job but in our faith, God gives us the spirit of power, love and a disciplined, sound mind. The importance of a sound mind in policing is unquestioned. Without a sound mind, policing in the split second moments of life would be impossible. Lt. Colonel David Grossman has developed an entire series based on the "Bullet-proof mind", preparing our minds for the difficult task of policing. This is completely compatible with the directions we have through faith in a God who desires to give us the sound mind needed for the role of both servant and warrior. Cowardice can have no part of the role we have in law enforcement. The shame that is there for those who don't do the job because they are afraid would be unbearable for many and would likely result in the distrust of their peers. In my early days of policing, I believe this is what motivated the one officer to say he wouldn't work with me. He had a false belief that because of my faith, I would be too afraid to use my weapon to kill someone if it came down to it. He had a belief about Christian people that was not warranted. The truth of the matter is, God can give us a sound mind, power and love to do the job with confidence and without fear – fear of man or fear of God.

As officers, we must be able to make sound decisions and choices in the face of difficulty. This was a characteristic that Inspector Jim Sneep emphasized strongly. He says, "A peace officer must have the ability to translate training into action without significant passion so as to have clear thinking ability under duress. He must make relevant prudent choices under fire, like a machine when the bullets fly."

Jim Amsing credits a sound mind from his faith when he had to make a very quick decision one day that nearly took the life of an innocent young high school student. He was called to a robbery in progress in the downtown core. A person in a black trench coat was holding up a Subway restaurant. He was very close and responded immediately. Normally he would have stayed back and set up on the place but he was able to get in very close to the store without being seen. The bad guy backed out of the store and didn't see Jim. Jim had his gun drawn and was prepared to fire if the bad guy raised his rifle in Jim's direction or anyone else's for that matter. Suddenly he had a sense that he could grab this guy and slam him to the ground without using his gun. He grabbed the suspect by the head and slammed him into the sidewalk, disarmed him and was able to handcuff and detain the suspect very quickly. When he turned the guy over, it turns out it was a girl and eventually they discovered that this so-called robbery was actually a school video that they were shooting and hadn't told anyone about it. A sound decision, based in Jim's belief in God's ability to direct him, resulted in a sore but alive young lady who could have been dead. The teacher from the school was severely reprimanded for not notifying police of their actions.

The ability of the mind to make sound decisions is often based on two things, knowledge and wisdom. Knowledge is the information that we have about circumstances, systems, skills and people that gives us understanding. Wisdom however is the ability to use that information to hopefully achieve a desired outcome in a correct manner. The book of Proverbs has been used by people in all walks of life to gain wisdom and knowledge about many of life's topics.

Proverbs 1:7 says, "The fear of the Lord is the beginning of knowledge but fools despise wisdom and discipline." I take this verse to mean that if we are to gain true knowledge it must begin with a reverential awe of God that recognizes that He is the source of all knowledge. He is the creator and designer of all things. When we in our faith come to that understanding, we will first look to God's understanding before we jump to conclusions based on our own limited knowledge.

We live in a time when the amount of knowledge available to us is completely overwhelming. Police services have policy manuals several times thicker than most university text books and as officers we are required to have all this knowledge in our grasp. Then we have all the court decisions that change policy and procedures on an on-going, ever-changing basis. At any given time we are supposed to know how to stop an arterial bleed, fix a loose bicycle chain for a child, understand the complexities of skid coefficients at an accident scene, soothe the ache of a mother who just lost her child to SIDS, prevent a suicidal individual from jumping off a parkade roof, then return to the office and sort through 50-100 emails with more information. And the list goes on.

At some point we have to discern what knowledge is important to us because we can't possibly know it all. This is where I believe understanding the fear of the Lord comes in. It has been my experience and the experience of many other officers of faith that when the information is needed at a given time, God can provide the information needed.

I recall one difficult investigation that I was involved in where we were trying to locate a known culprit. He had managed to escape our grasp for several weeks. I knew who his friends were, where he liked to hang out, and the kinds of vehicles he liked to steal or drive. I had a plethora of information about him but not much seemed to work in finding him, until one day out of desperation more than faith . . . I asked God what to do next. Out of the blue, I had a sense that we were supposed to go to a mobile home park at the south end of town. I jumped into an unmarked vehicle with my partner and started driving around in the area of the mobile park. Sure enough, out of the alley comes our bad guy in a stolen truck similar to those he'd stolen before. The chase was on. For safety reasons (we were in a heavily populated area), we called off the chase, one of his partners in crime got out on foot and ran. We caught him and as a result we were able to gain all the information we needed to complete the case, locate and charge this bad guy and obtain a conviction in court. This all came because I believe God gave me a sense of knowledge that I did not have before that I was able to act upon.

I have talked to numerous officers of faith who have shared very similar stories with the same kinds of results. Now I realize that many other officers who are not of faith have had similar stories; they would say it was simply coincidence or intuition but I have come to see these more as God-incidents than co-incidences because I believe God intervenes for His own sake of justice and righteousness. God himself is a God of justice and desires to see the bad guys held accountable for His own sake.

Another area of the mind is the use of wisdom. Wisdom is applied knowledge. Listen to the words of one of the wisest men who ever lived, King Solomon.

Proverbs 2

1   My son, if you receive my words,
And treasure my commands within you,

2   So that you incline your ear to wisdom,
And apply your heart to understanding;

3   Yes, if you cry out for discernment,
And lift up your voice for understanding,

4   If you seek her as silver,
And search for her as for hidden treasures;

5   Then you will understand the fear of the Lord,
And find the knowledge of God.

6 For the Lord gives wisdom;
  From His mouth come knowledge and
  understanding;

7 He stores up sound wisdom for the upright;
  He is a shield to those who walk uprightly;

8 He guards the paths of justice,
  And preserves the way of His saints.

9 Then you will understand righteousness and justice,
  Equity and every good path.

10 When wisdom enters your heart,
  And knowledge is pleasant to your soul,

11 Discretion will preserve you;
  Understanding will keep you,

12 To deliver you from the way of evil,
  From the man who speaks perverse things,

13 From those who leave the paths of uprightness
  To walk in the ways of darkness;

14 Who rejoice in doing evil,
  And delight in the perversity of the wicked;

15 Whose ways are crooked,
  And who are devious in their paths;

16 To deliver you from the immoral woman,
  From the seductress who flatters with her words,

17 Who forsakes the companion of her youth,
  And forgets the covenant of her God.

18 For her house leads down to death,
  And her paths to the dead;

19 None who go to her return,
  Nor do they regain the paths of life—

20 So you may walk in the way of goodness,
  And keep to the paths of righteousness.

21 For the upright will dwell in the land,

And the blameless will remain in it;

22   But the wicked will be cut off from the earth,

And the unfaithful will be uprooted from it.

The wisdom of Proverbs should be sought after like gold and silver. It provides guidance for life, instruction for understanding, sound discernment for making wise choices, seeing good from evil and knowing when to avoid and when to engage. Wisdom leads to the knowledge of God and seeing Him active in our lives as officers.

Wisdom is essential to making a good cop. Because of the diverse situations, circumstances, people and problems we as officers face, we need the wisdom of God to assist us in making those sound decisions in quick order. God encourages us to ask Him for His wisdom for the times we lack it. Knowing how to use all the information that we have, makes for wisdom.

I worked with one of Calgary finest detectives who showed me some tricks of the trade that came from his wisdom and understanding of people and their criminal behaviors. We were working on the case of a large group of people who were shop-lifting literally millions of dollars worth of product each year. They had set up their own underground stores to peddle the stolen merchandise. A "Crime-Stoppers" tip came in and using this information, this detective knew from his experience that these people would likely throw the store tags in the garbage. We waited and found several garbage bags left in the back alley by the suspect's residence. We took these back to the office and sifted through and found several thousand dollars' worth of store tags. With this information, the Crime Stoppers tip and some back-ground history on the suspects, we were able to obtain a search warrant which led to the recovery of thousands of dollars' worth of stolen clothing, household appliances and stereo equipment, all shoplifted or stolen in break-and-enters. This led to a much larger investigation which led to the breaking up, at least for a while, of a large shoplifting ring and the imprisonment of several of the ringleaders. All because an experienced detective knew how to use the knowledge he had in wise ways.

The importance of the mind and its control over many aspects of our lives must be considered. The cynical mind of the cynical cop leads to depression and poor functioning as a servant warrior. If wisdom is to be sought after and fear of the Lord leads to knowledge, then the mind must also focus on the right things so that cynicism doesn't rule. A positive attitude changes a person's whole disposition. As an officer, I gained a cynical attitude about many people and to this day I am still more critical than I'd like to be. To help me combat that, I have a statement that I keep posted as part of my life journey that says this, "Finally, brothers, whatever is true, whatever is noble, whatever is right, whatever is pure, whatever is lovely, whatever is admirable – if anything is excellent or praiseworthy – think about such things.....and the God of peace will be with you." (Phil. 4:8)

Despite the fact that many of people we deal with out there have real issues that can cause cynicism, a far greater majority are good people. These things are worth remembering and celebrating. We especially need to remember the true, noble, admirable, praiseworthy and excellent so we can keep from falling into the pit of cynicism. This is a choice we must make of our will and not of our emotions.

Reading is another aspect of growing in our knowledge and wisdom in this role as a servant warrior. Sadly I know too many officers who don't read on a regular basis because they say they are just too busy or there is too much policy to read already. Many years ago, I decided to read at least twelve books a year. I have been able to keep to that for the most part and in fact most years read far more than twelve. Reading has helped me to see the world from a much broader perspective and improve my own world view. I have the opportunity to learn from other's lives and mistakes to gain wisdom for the job in front of me. I am reminded that I am not alone in this world and I don't have all the answers.

As officers of faith we must always remember to have an attitude or mind focused on humility. Though Jesus himself was God, he didn't hang on to that and demand that people treat him like God but rather he came as a servant, took a servant's posture even to the point of death for the sake of many. As a result, God raised him up and gave him a name recognized around the world. I believe God will do the same for us. If we as officers remember that we are not God, as Sgt. Terry Larson once said, and act as servants with humble attitudes, God will raise us up and celebrate us. We won't have to, He'll do it. The choice to use our will in a humble positive way, will keep us out of cynicism.

The will of man is another component of the mind that has been referred to a few times already and needs some emphasis. The will is a very powerful thing and as officers we are encouraged to use the power of the will to overcome. There are many stories of officers who have faced being shot and have willed themselves to survive.

I had the privilege of meeting Officer Bobby Smith, a Louisiana State Trooper who was shot in the face and eyes at point blank range twice. He survived that shooting in many respects because he willed himself to live and not give up. He was blinded by that event but now has gone on to get his doctorate and teaches police officers throughout United States and Canada. His story is really quite amazing. He also gives credit to his faith in God for helping him to recover and have the strength of will to continue on through a great struggle to recover. As a result God has used him greatly to benefit many other officers.

Colonel David Grossman has written about the "bullet-proof mind" so that officers can have the strength of will to survive almost any difficult situation and make sound decisions, experiencing courage in the face of death. The mind must make the choice to will itself to survive and fight through the adversity. I had that experience once and it both scared me and strengthened me. I was canoeing with my father on the Athabasca River in Alberta. We had tipped over a couple of times in the frigid waters and I had gotten cold and exhibited signs of hypothermia. We were in the middle of the river in good-sized rapids when we capsized again. This time I was a long way from the shore and was being carried down the river. I was getting very cold, had hit my head on the canoe when it capsized and was a bit disoriented. For a period of time, I had this sense that I could die in this water and had a feeling of giving up to it. This scared the crap out of me because I had never experienced that willingness to give up to death before. At that point, my will kicked in and I began to swim to the canoe, grabbed it by the gunnels and began to fight to get to the shore. My father had managed to hang onto the canoe of some friends we were with and as a result we were able to get to shore as a gravel bar approached as we rounded a corner in the river. I pulled myself and the canoe out of the water and bent over, stunned at what had just happened to me. Not because I had tipped over in the frigid waters but because I had a moment where I thought death would have me. Fortunately the good Lord has other plans for me and I was able to will myself out of it and swim to safety. The power of the will both to give in and to survive surprised me. A "bullet-proof mind" can help you to survive.

The last aspect of the mind is the emotions. This is a sorely neglected part of the police officer and I am thankful for men like Dr. Kevin Gilmartin who are addressing the issues of emotions in police officers. Two other men that have led the way in dealing with the emotional state of those in the emergency services field are Jeffery Mitchell and George Everly who founded the International Critical Incident Stress Foundation. These two men recognized the huge emotional impact that major critical incidents have on first responders and devised a method for helping officers deal effectively with the normal reactions to extremely abnormal events.

Critical Incident Stress Management has become a significant and effective way for peace officers to deal with the emotional damage that occurs when they are faced with overwhelming events like the death of an officer or a plane crash or when dealing with an accumulation of significant events over time such as repeated fatal car accidents, homicides, particularly where children are involved, or any other series of events that can overwhelm the soul of an officer.

CISM, as it is referred to, involved several processes that all deal with educating officers about the physical, mental, emotional and spiritual effects that these events can have on people. Secondly, it provides an arena whereby officers can vent in a healthy environment with peers and/or mental health professionals so as to recognize the emotional impact a particular event has had on an officer.

I have had the privilege of being involved in the training and participation with many officers in dealing appropriately with the emotional impact of policing. It has been a very rewarding experience. One aspect of this that I have found encouraging is the willingness of senior officers to verbalize how they were impacted emotionally by a traumatic event. In nearly every case I've dealt with, the senior officers opened up quite naturally and willingly. This encouraged the younger officers, who are still learning to deal with the macho, tough-guy image of policing, to open up and express how they were impacted by the event.

This has almost always been very cathartic and beneficial to all involved and helped reduce the impact over the long haul.

There is an old saying that confession is good for the soul. I believe that this kind of confession, if you like, really does help with the emotional state of officers. In terms of faith in policing, confession is a necessary part of healing and recovery. The term confession simply means "to be in agreement with", to openly acknowledge that this is my state of being. There is no denial of our state but rather recognition that this is where I am at. The confession of our emotion is not a bad thing and allows for the recognition and effective dealing with what I am experiencing at this time. It is the denial of where I am at emotionally that causes the most significant problems for officers and ultimately their families. Often it is the deep and usually untrue fears of rejection that come if I admit that this is what I am experiencing emotionally. That is why it is so good to hear senior guys and gals admit publicly that they had various emotions that often are not admitted within the police world.

So what does faith have to do with this? Our willingness to admit to God, who cares deeply about us and knows the impact that the world's evil has on us, in an honest way can lead to maintaining or restoring our emotional health. When we confess our state to Him, He can begin to bring healing to our spiritual and emotional lives, both maintaining and restoring our health.

I love the book of Psalms in the Bible because for the most part these passages are expressions of David and others of their emotional state before God. David often describes his anger at God, his feelings of being abandoned, his loneliness, his fear about the enemy but he always acknowledges that somehow God is in charge. God honored David's honest expressions to Him and said that of all men, David's heart was after God. God's heart resonated with David's heart because he was honest with who he was in relationship to God. Nothing was hidden. As a result, David became the greatest king of Israel and out of David's lineage came the Christ, Jesus. This is a great honor to a man who was honest about his emotions.

I believe that faith is important in policing because it is our honest confession before God of what we hate, what angers us, our deep frustration with "the system" and what we love that keeps us well and prevents us from falling deeply into cynicism. Confession is good for the soul and invites us to a deeper, healthier lifestyle that allows us to continue to minister to hurting people in a hurting world.

2. The Body

As I indicated in my introduction to this chapter, the physical training for the job of policing has often been the most fun aspect of the career. The idea of maintaining our physical being has been driven home and is considered extremely important by all. I think frequently of the picture found in fitness facilities that reminds me that the bad guys are working out constantly at the prison gyms and as an officer I'd better be prepared myself. Training the body to respond immediately to situations gone bad is vitally important, to the point of life or death. To train the hand, eye, finger and muscles to respond automatically with our handguns has been part of my training personally for many years. I wanted to know that I could draw and fire my weapon from virtually any position and know that my body would react and respond without thinking about the motions required.

As officers of faith we are encouraged and invited by God to train ourselves well. I think of the story of David and Goliath in the Bible. Here is a small shepherd boy who is willing to take on a nine-foot giant of a man when all the other soldiers of Israel were too afraid. What made David different? Two things! Most importantly, it was his faith in his God to give him victory because God had proved himself to David in the past, and it was his physical practice with his weapon of choice that gave him the skills to carry out the task of taking down the giant. David had become so skilled in his use of the sling that he was deadly accurate, knew his weapon and knew the kinds of smooth stones he needed to give him success. When David took on Goliath he had already killed a bear and a lion in protecting the sheep so he knew that with God's help and his trained arm he could take on this threatening giant. And he did.

In another passage of the Bible, Paul encourages his protégé to endure hardship like a good soldier who doesn't get himself wrapped up in matters that are not important to him but tries to please the one whom he serves. He encourages him to train as an athlete would, according to the rules so that he can win the prize he was called to win. We too as officers must prepare ourselves and train according to the rules laid out before us so that we can win the battles and essentially please those we work for. Any athlete must train physically for the challenge and officers must train physically for the challenge they have as well, not just physically but emotionally as well.

We are also encouraged to see our physical bodies as the physical temple of God. Many passages in the Bible refer to the presence of God dwelling in those that have faith in Him. He describes us as being the temple. As a result we need to treat our body with respect and not abuse it but rather care for it as a representative of where God has chosen to live. I take this to mean we need to be careful about the things we eat and how much or how little we eat. It also means making sure the body gets enough rest.

Rest can often be an extremely difficult thing to regulate for peace officers. We are frequently called to work overtime on cases and attend court during our night shift which obviously reduces the number of hours of sleep available to us. Many will get called out in the middle of the night to handle homicides, traffic deaths and the like. Officers will take on extra duties to supplement their income and often don't take time off during the week to recover. This is very unhealthy. Are we somehow better than God? Even God rested after six days of work to look back and reflect on what He had created. He saw what He did was good and took time to appreciate what He'd done. It was also a day to rest and physically recover so the body could take on the next week. The Sabbath day was a day to celebrate and enjoy community, doing something completely unrelated to the labor of the week. The rest day was also a time to reflect on the deeper, more important dreams we have.

The important and urgent	The important but not urgent
Not important and urgent	Not important and not urgent

I have always appreciated the book, *Seven Habits of Highly Effective People* by Steve Covey. He established a time box in relationship to our important tasks vs our unimportant tasks.[19] He describes getting caught up in the tyranny of the urgent where we are constantly responding to immediate needs. As a result, the important goals and dreams of our life get shoved to the side and rarely get a chance to be looked at. If we do not take the time to rest, we don't get reflect and decide whether we are doing the important things in life or just in auto-pilot, responding to life rather than living life. Cops are notorious for this. We get so caught up in the urgent and important at work and the not important and not urgent at home that the real things that matter, our dreams and hopes for ourselves and our families, get left out or forgotten.

Taking the time to properly rest allows us to reflect on the creative work done, where we are going so we can make course corrections as needed, celebrate life with our families and friends and physically rest our bodies so they can continue to work. I am not saying that this is a Sabbath day law. That is simply impractical for law enforcement but we should have our own Sabbath day rule that we do what we can to keep. Here are some suggestions for resting taken from "CrossWalk.com"

a. Begin by honestly exploring the question: "What does rest look like for you?" For some, rest and renewal means curling up with a book for an entire day; for others, it's hiking the toughest trail you can find or wandering the halls of a local museum. Before making any plans, make a clear, concise list of activities that genuinely lead you to rest and renewal.

b. Design a Rule of Life for rest and renewal. A Rule of Life is a regular spiritual practice that a person adopts as sacred and nonnegotiable. For example, spending time meditating on Scripture each morning could be part of a person's Rule of Life, or taking Sunday as a nonnegotiable day of rest and renewal. Based on your list of genuinely restful activities, design a Rule of Life for rest and renewal that sounds inviting to you, and try it out for a few weeks. Take a playful approach with this. If something doesn't work the way you'd hoped, don't get frustrated about it. Instead, just drop it and try something else. This is a process of discovery. In time, you will find a Rule of Life that works best for you.

c. Tell your family and close friends about your Rule of Life for rest and renewal. Explain that the Rule is nonnegotiable, and invite them to help you stay committed to your practice of regular withdrawal and rest.[20]

The importance of taking care of our physical bodies is clearly supported by God and His word to us. We need to be prepared physically to handle the servant warrior role through exercise and physical training. We are encouraged and invited to be the best servant warrior we can be, prepared to fight the good fight. We also need to know when to rest and reflect so we can stay on the course God has set before us, including the pursuit of our dreams that God Himself has likely put there. Proper rest and reflection will help us become far more effective officers and family members in the day-to-day work of life.

3. The Spirit

Caring for the spiritual side of the law enforcement officer is probably the greatest reason why I have written this book. This is one of the most neglected areas of law enforcement, yet it is, in my opinion, the most vital aspect of who we are, what we do and how we do what we do. To know that we are the beloved of God, sons and daughters of the King, that our task and calling is divinely appointed and that He has given us all the authority and tools we need to carry out His purposes is profound and has eternal consequences for mankind now and into eternity. Yet we do little if anything to care for the spirit and soul of man.

Several years ago, I went to see Jean Vanier, the son of one of Canada's Governor Generals. He established a ministry in Canada and in France that served the severely mentally or physically handicapped people. He set up homes where physically well people would live in community with the handicapped. This ministry is called L'Arche Ministries. What he had to say at this conference has impacted me to this day. What he found was that the physically and mentally handicapped had a profound ability to love and be loved and though their bodies and minds may be broken they were indeed the beloved of God. He also said that it caused those who were physically well to recognize their own spiritual and emotional brokenness in the presence of the handicapped; it caused them to see themselves also as the beloved of God.

This past year, I read a small book containing the writings of Henri Nouwen, a priest in the Catholic Church, called *Spiritual Direction; Wisdom for the Long Walk of Faith*. Nouwen had been a professor at Harvard and Yale Universities and, by all appearances to the world, was an extremely successful teacher and profound writer. Yet he discovered that he too was broken and needed healing. He ended up in Canada at one of the L'Arche community houses where he cared for one of the residents. During this time he came to understand that in the midst of his brokenness, he was greatly loved and more importantly that he was the beloved of God.

I believe strongly that all of us are broken individuals in some very deep places in our lives. Yet in our brokenness we find out that we are the deeply beloved of God. I need to quote Henri Nouwen on the point.

> "We all have wounds. We all live in pain and disappointment. We all have feelings of loneliness that lurk beneath all our successes, feelings of uselessness that hide under all the praise, feeling of meaninglessness even when people say we are fantastic – and this is what makes us sometimes grab onto people and expect from them affections, affirmation and love that they cannot give."[21]

Nouwen's point is that only God can love us the way people cannot. In policing we are constantly looking to our spouses, police partners, supervisors and management to say how good we are and approve of our performances, give us the at-a-boys, promotions, specialty units and on and on it goes. Until we as law enforcement see that we are in fact broken people, we will not see our need for God and to be seen as His Beloved.

That is one of the most profound things about caring for the soul and spirit of the peace officer: knowing that God really does approve of us, that we are His sons and daughters, that we hold a special place in His heart and that we really are His Beloved. It is only from this point that we can go out and serve the community, live in the community and maybe even die for the community without the selfish expectation that somehow they must meet our needs of belonging, meaning and purpose. They can't....only God can.

So how do we care for the spirit of the law enforcement officer? It isn't easy, particularly because we are very action-oriented people. For us it is very much, "Do on Do, Do on Do, Rule on Rule, Rule on Rule" (Isaiah 28:13). We usually must be doing something or we feel useless and out of control. So I am going to suggest that doing the opposite of doing is how we take care of our own spirit.

1. We need to be still and recognize and know
   that God is God. We need to stop and reflect
   on who He is and who we are in relationship to
   Him. Psalm 46 is where this comes from.

I had an interesting experience over this passage recently. In my retirement, I am still trying to accomplish my dreams and goals and so seldom let up on God. In my quiet time, I was always telling God what I wanted to do and would He let me do this or that particularly when it came to looking for or buying land to build a guest ranch for peace officers. In my quiet times I know that God had told me I was to do two things. One was to finish this book and the other was to get my house ready for sale when the time came. I kept saying "yeah but..." and listing my desires again and again. Finally one morning after many failed attempts to get God to pay attention to my demands, I distinctly heard Him and figuratively felt Him grabbed me by the shirt collar, pull me up close and say....."SHUT UP! I told you to do two things, finish your book and finish your house. Don't bug Me until you're finished that, then we'll talk about the future." I got the message. I am to do only what I was told to do then rest in the knowing He was in charge. I'm a little slow though and it took God getting in my face to wake up and be still.

As peace officers we need to find the places to be still and know God is God. It is here that we will discover that we are the Beloved. For many, that place could be quietly fishing along a river or lake. It could be hiking in the mountains. It could be sitting quietly in a favourite chair reading.

A mentor friend gave me some verses to meditate on that helped me quite a bit. "In repentance and rest is your salvation; in quietness and trust is your strength." (Isaiah 30:15) We all need to make space for God in our souls. Solitude is really one of the few places where we can connect with God and be restored and strengthened for the task ahead. Though we are often trying to find God in the daily busyness of life, God finds us when we stop and are quiet long enough to listen instead of incessantly talking. I think it was Martin Luther King who once said, "I have so much to do today, that I have to spend two hours quietly before God to get any of it done."

2. Being still and quiet before God in places of silence and solitude is one way we can care for our
   spirit and know that we are the Beloved of God.We

need to be in healthy community relationships.

When I say healthy I mean relationships that don't <u>demand</u> that we be approved of, find meaning in, or purpose behind. I would like to quote Henri Nouwen again. He is talking about the role of forgiveness as a function of healthy community.

> "Within the discipline of life in community are the twin gifts of forgiveness and celebration that need to be opened and used regularly. What is forgiveness? Forgiveness means that I continually am willing to forgive the other person for not fulfilling all my needs and desires. Forgiveness says, "I know you love me, but you don't have to love me unconditionally because only God can do that." I too must ask forgiveness for not being able to fulfill other people's total needs, <u>for no human being can do that.</u>" [22] (emphasis mine).

Relationships where we are demanding to be cared for or the other is demanding to be cared for are unhealthy and need to be avoided as they drain us and do not restore us. It is too much like the continued work on the street where we are being sucked dry by the demands of people on our ability to rescue them, fix their problems, or the other guy's problem.

To that end, I encourage officers to find healthy relationships from within their peers and peer families. We all need people that we can relate to, that understand the difficulties of our journey as law enforcement. Our spouses often need people who understand their roles as spouses and the unique stressors that are there for them and us. This helps us to feel that we are not alone in this difficult world and that others do understand.

I would also encourage officers to find an older officer who will mentor them. Mentoring is so underrated these days because we are generally very independent people and feel we don't need anyone else. This just isn't true. Having someone who can guide us along the law enforcement journey is so important. I personally have sought a spiritual director who guides me in my relationship with God. I mentioned earlier that I had older supervisors who mentored me. I will always be grateful for them.

It is vitally important to have healthy relationships outside of the peace officer community. Life is far more than our professions and we need to see good people doing good things to improve our world view and see that not everyone is against us. Working with great young people as a school resource officer and with community leaders as a community liaison officer helped me to see so many good people out there that really support us. We need friendship like this as well. This will help protect us from the "us vs. them" mentality.

We need to find others who are of the same faith as we are, to do as Nouwen said, practice forgiveness and celebration. We need people who will journey with us in our relationship towards God and others. We need to be able to celebrate life in those moments where we rest from our labors. It is fun to celebrate what we've done and to celebrate what they have done together. It helps us to dream more in community and see what can be accomplished in the greater scheme of things. Nouwen points out very accurately that we must be able to move from a place of knowing we are the beloved of God into a community where we express the celebration of being mutually the beloved of God. This in turn helps us to love God even more.

We need to be in ministry.

Jesus said that all the rules and all the laws of man and God could be filtered down into two things: Love the Lord your God with all your heart, mind, soul and strength; and love your neighbor as yourself. When we are in a place where we know that we are beloved of God and we can share this with others who understand, we are almost compelled to move this out into a place where we'd like others to experience being the beloved of God as well. This becomes the expression of being the hands and feet of God to others.

Bono of the rock band U2 is a modern-day example of a guy who knows he's loved of God, doesn't follow the traditional "churchy" route, yet as an expression of being the beloved has helped found the ONE campaign aimed at ending what he calls "stupid poverty". His goal is to eliminate third world debt and provide for the poor in a generation that like never before has the ability to feed the truly hungry and fight AIDS.

One of the greatest personal accomplishments for myself and my wife Deborah over the past year and a half was serving in Gulfport, Mississippi with twenty four other peace officers, firemen and civilians who went down to help officers and firefighters who lost absolutely everything to Hurricane Katrina. We served because we wanted to and we made a significant difference in at least three families' lives because we chose to serve. We did not ask for anything in return, simply the opportunity to serve them. Yet our spirits were lifted up as never before and we enjoyed very hard work but often laughed our heads off in the midst of it, thoroughly enjoying the people we served and who we served with.

See your role as a peace officer as an opportunity to serve. This isn't just a job; it's a calling and a divine appointment. God approves of you, He authorizes you to do the work of justice and He will empower you to do it. Love God. Love others. There is no higher calling.

Chapter Eight
The Servant Warrior at Home

The Home front.... aawww, ...the home front. It is the place of rest and solace for the weary warrior after a day or night in battle. A Toronto police officer, Anthony Saldutto, painted a picture of the officer having just arrived home still in his uniform. He slumps into his favorite chair, slides into a comfortable position and promptly takes a nap. His adoring children are gathered around him, waiting and watching while his loving, doting wife watches the children from the kitchen. The perfect picture of the perfect home front.

Unfortunately, as you'd probably guess, that is seldom the way it really is. One of the practices my wife and I did follow was to allow me a short nap after I came home from day shift so I could relax before joining the family for supper. This helped me tremendously to unwind and reenter the home front with a more ready and willing heart. However most of the time there wasn't the opportunity to unwind and reconnect, it was usually right into the swing of things or off to bed or wait for morning court to come around. The more likely scenario for most officers is to arrive home and sit in the easy chair with a remote control in hand or mouse for the computer and zone out. The family usually gets ignored and great effort must be put in by the spouse to gain the momentary attention of the exhausted officer.

Early in our marriage and my career in law enforcement, Deborah and I went through a particularly difficult time. I mentioned my struggle in my identity and how I was fitting in as an officer and a Christian. I would be very much up and alert for work but would come home and be quite sullen and withdrawn. Due to our own immaturity and individual struggles, this caused Deborah to feel that she had done something wrong in our relationship and to come across as demanding and frustrated. I wasn't talking to her and she thought she was the problem. The truth was, the job was the problem. I was struggling with what I was experiencing in the job and withdrew. This resulted in numerous fights and arguments. It was easier to stay at work or away from home and not have to deal with the home front. Being at home was just too uncomfortable. Deborah felt unloved and ignored. I felt disrespected and misunderstood.

The results of all this on the police marriage is devastating. Many do not work through the problems that arise due to the priority given to the job, which results in very high rates of divorce and deeply wounded individuals and children. Although statistics are hard to find on the divorce rate in the law enforcement field, anecdotal evidence seems to suggest that 66%-85% of marriages will end in divorce. I worked on several teams where easily two-thirds of the team were divorced. On one team of 12 members, only myself and one other member were still married to the same wives we'd started with. Many of the chaplain's conferences in Canada and the United States speak with despair about an unusually high divorce rate of 75-90%. We don't fully know what it is but we do know that marriage is taking a beating in the law enforcement field. It doesn't have to be this way.

When I did my interviews with spouses and officers across the country, one of the most common themes was how the job became so much more important to the officer than the family or so it would seem. Overtime, court, shift work, call out and often just the plain excitement of the job would take officers away from their family for long hours. One spouse said, "Work comes before family and everything else. Police officers can have a misguided feeling of self importance. Once the uniform is put on they feel they have all the power and are in charge of all. No one else can take care of situations and they must control all situations." For many this also means at home too. Her officer husband said, "Being a police officer sucks the life out of a person because it is never-ending woe out there. It's hard to reconcile doing good yet not being able to help anyone. Our marriage has been affected by a lack of attention to my wife, because of the demands of the profession. I consciously pulled back from some "me" things and tried for more "us" things."

I have compiled a summary of the concerns and problems that arose for the officers and spouses so as to have an overview of what to expect in the law enforcement marriage. These are the issues identified by the officers and spouses:

1. Hyper-vigilance cycle
    1.a Up at work, down at home
    1.b Communicate at work, don't communicate at home.
    1.c Cynical and apathetic at home and work
    1.d Capable at work but feeling hopeless and defeated at home
    1.e Depression or sadness
    1.f Identity wrapped up in the badge.
2. Police personality

2.a   Anger

2.b   Control oriented – affects spouse and children

2.c   Rigid uncompromising personality

2.d   Pride and macho image – unwilling to change decision due to pride and image

2.e   High expectations of people – more absolutes

     2.e.i Wife

     2.e.ii children

2.f   Problem solvers – jump to conclusions at home

2.g   Fact oriented and less compassionate

     2.g.i Emotionally detached

     2.g.ii aloof

2.h   Loves excitement and risk taking

3. Over commitment to work

3.a   Family events cancelled

3.b   Social life limited

     3.b.i Too tired to go out

     3.b.ii Only police related friends

3.c   Lack of balance in and around priorities

3.d   Being a single parent

3.e   Living separate lives

4. Addictive patterns

4.a   Alcohol

4.b   Sexual

4.c   Prescription drugs

5. Work Related Stressors

5.a   Critical Incident Stress

5.b   Post Traumatic Stress Disorder

5.c   Time pressures – court, overtime, shifts

5.d   Parenting due to shifts – keeping children quiet

5.e   Internal politics - more stress
6. Communication

6.a   With anger

6.b   Negativity

6.c   Impatience

6.d   Not talking – lack of understanding about
what is occurring in each others lives

6.e   Withdrawn into self

As you can see I broke these concerns down into larger categories to identify common themes that arose for these married officers and their spouses. With some exceptions the hyper-vigilance cycle, the police personality, over commitment to work, addictive behaviors, work related stressors, and communications were the significant show stoppers in marriage. I would like to discuss these issues and give examples of how they impacted the marriages. I then would like offer solutions that were offered to me by the officers and spouses.

Hyper-vigilance

Dr. Kevin Gilmartin probably describes what happens best in his book, *Emotional Survival for Law Enforcement.* According to Gilmartin, the officer goes through cycles when he is working. When he goes to work he is at a very high state of alertness and readiness. He is attentive, humorous, communicative and ready for action. We call this state "hyper-vigilance". The officer must be in this high state of alertness because of the demands of the job and the threat to his life or his partners if he fails to be fully aware during his shift. The officer is usually at his/her best. I have referred to this state earlier in the book.

What happens when the officer comes home is the opposite! Generally speaking the officer will withdraw, struggle to communicate, lose the sense of humor, be barely conscious and easily tune out spouse and children. Unless events are well planned in advance, it would be a struggle to get back out the door to attend functions. Now this isn't the case with all officers but it is generally very common.

A couple of years ago, my wife and I attended a Police Leadership training conference in Vancouver, BC where Gilmartin was the guest speaker. I sat at the back and watched the reactions of the officers in the room. Heads were nodding in total affirmation. When the session was over, the most common theme I heard was, "Man! That is me!" Deborah and I giggled because we could totally relate. These were men and women of all ranks within various police services and all could relate to what had just been spoken out loud.

Several members I spoke with said that they did not give their wives the attention they needed when they returned home from duty if they returned home at all. "People I've worked with seemed to only live for work. They'd come to work, and then work overtime on arrests they'd get just before shift end, then go off to court and maybe go home to sleep so they could get back to work." These words from one officer didn't surprise me in the least. I'd seen much the same over and over again. Spouses most definitely got the leftovers. The only time the officers felt up, was when they were working. Going home was more difficult. This officer then said, "They were emotional cripples." A very strong statement about the role hyper-vigilance played in the lives of these officers. When hyper-vigilance makes the job your sole identity, emotional unwellness is the result.

Another area where hyper-vigilance played a role was in developing some forms of sadness or depression which of course has its affects on the home and spouse. Inspector Sneep spoke of constantly dealing with human tragedy that left him and others with a sense of helplessness and lack of control over the entire career. This leads to a form of depression.

Years ago I spent a good deal of time with a member who had unfortunately taken another man's life because his dog did not respond the way he'd been trained. This human tragedy took a significant toll on this young man. His identity was very much wrapped up in his role as an officer and with this tragedy came a significant sadness that he was not able to recover from, at least not during the time I knew him. His wife was deeply affected by his sadness and despite her best efforts could not help him. She felt desperate and asked for my assistance as a friend. In the end, despite professional help, he had to leave the job, lost his wife and ended up moving away from his support systems. Identity and depression found through this hyper-vigilance cycle took away a once good officer.

The Police Personality

There is a definite police personality if you talk to anyone in the business and it impacts home greatly. Several years ago, the Calgary Police Service was doing an analysis of the police family and personalities and did a personality study on the members and some of the spouses. The study through the learning center showed that approximately 80% of the members were ISTJ or ESTJ on the Meyer-Briggs personality profile with 20% making up the difference spread throughout the personality types. I or E stood for introvert or extrovert, S represented sensing, T, thinking and J, judging. The common theme is that police officer live through their senses – sight, touch, hearing, taste, smell. They are fact based. Just the facts ma'am, just the facts. They are also thinking people who are able to process quickly and make quick decisions and sound judgments in short order. They love action and get bored quickly. They are take-charge kind of people who are quick to come up with solutions and solve problems. In a crisis you want this kind of people around.

This however doesn't go over so well at home unless the partners have been able to adjust over time to this lifestyle and allow the best of both partners to come out in their family decisions. Oftentimes this personality comes into conflict with spouses who are much more feeling oriented and compassionate. They aren't always looking for a solution, just an opportunity to talk and relate. Most officers just want to solve the problem and get on with it. Spouses don't feel heard or understood and when the officer doesn't talk because of the hyper-vigilance issues, then communication can break down quickly.

Children can find themselves being interrogated instead of cared for. I can remember many times when I found out one of my kids did something wrong and the interrogation and investigation would begin. I remember one particular time when a neighbor came to our house accusing our kids of pooping in a pan and leaving it in her backyard. Deborah and I were horrified. Well, the investigation began. I began questioning the kids about where they had been and at what time. Who had been over to her house? Where did the pan come from? Was it ours? Was it theirs? Finally, I discovered my boys had been over there and the interrogation began. Deborah pulled me aside and reminded me that the boys weren't criminals and I needed to knock it off. By this time, I'd scared the boys and had them all upset. They kept denying that they had done anything and I didn't believe them. After all, why would a neighbor come over and make such an allegation if it wasn't true? Well as it turned out, the neighbor discovered it was her own son and came some time later and apologized but unfortunately the damage had been done with my boys. They felt like they were the bad guys and I didn't help by my actions towards them. I had to apologize and I learned a valuable lesson that day about how the police officer in me needs to cool it around my kids. I also learned the valuable lesson about not judging situations too quickly without hearing all sides of the story without prejudice.

Deborah and I have also learned to live around the value of the police officer personality and appreciate what it does bring to the table. But it must be tempered with the strengths of the spouse's personality so that the real value of the cop mentality can be a benefit in the family and not a hindrance. What is most important to learn for both partners is the love and respect necessary to allow the personalities to train and benefit each other instead of clashing and fighting.

In courtship or dating, people love the strengths that each person brings to the relationship. However once married and living in close proximity to each other over a period of time, some of those strengths of personality are seen rather as weaknesses and annoyances, which causes strain in the marriage. In dating we are always presenting our best side and our partners rarely see the bad side of the personality traits. Thus the women love the strong, courageous, decisive macho police type and are drawn to this. The officer is drawn to the caring, compassionate, relational partner. After marriage, one can be seen as controlling and not listening, too quick to make decisions without the relational piece and the other is seen as weak and indecisive. Conflict begins. Through learning to love and respect each other, and if people are willing and don't bale too quickly, these traits can be seen as strengths again as they get tempered through the fires of adversity.

Over-commitment to Work

A significant issue for all the families I interviewed was over-commitment to work. Several spouses referred to the shift work causing them to feel like single parents. Officers were frequently required to work overtime because of the demands of paperwork associated with an arrest or search warrant. Added to this was the requirement of court, court preparation and desired special duties like football or hockey games or other cultural or musical events.

I spoke with a spouse recently whose husband was part of the homicide unit. The demands in homicide in recent months had been particularly strenuous due to some gang related murders. His time at home was extremely limited and sleep patterns were very erratic and short. He was tired and absent. I know this officer and I know his heart is not to be tired and absent, particularly for his family. He is truly a family man. He is a good dad and husband. He simply could not be home because the investigative work was exceedingly demanding. Victims' families were demanding and should be receiving good work on the part of the police service. This police family also has a child that has special needs. The spouse was feeling very much like a single woman and mom and was carrying the burden of her family almost alone. She was tired and feeling quite alone.

Unfortunately, this is quite typical for the police family and marriage. Frequently, spouses and officers commented on times when there were significant events occurring for the family that the officers had to miss due to overtime or being called out, particularly if they were attached to a specialty unit. The whole family is impacted by this and children, in particular. Sometimes children feel left out and in some way abandoned by the officer, male or female. Learning to deal with these disappointments is very important for the police family and marriage.

Members usually really enjoy the work of policing but struggle with the management and court. They actually like what they do and in the hyper-vigilance cycle, find it easier and more stimulating at work. If things aren't as good at home then it is far easier to stay at work.

I had a classmate in police training who echoed this very well. He was a very well respected officer and an expert in motorcycle gangs. He loved the stimulation and excitement of his job. He loved the challenge of getting inside the gangs and helping bring them down in whatever way possible. It was life-giving for him. He literally said he'd rather be at work doing this than being at home with his family and wife. He lived for the job.

One of the officers I interviewed lost his first marriage simply because he was too over-committed to his work. He said he learned his lesson the hard way and the second time around made his married life the first priority. His spouse confirmed that and they learned to adapt their time schedules to benefit each other according to the shifts they worked.

Over-commitment to work is a significant issue for the Servant Warrior at home.

Addictive Behaviours

When I joined the Calgary Police Service many years ago, it was normal practice for officers to head off to the Cuff and Billy (the association bar) for a few beers after work to "debrief" the day and enjoy the camaraderie of policing. This often led to excessive use of alcohol to deal with the stressors of the job. It also left the spouses at home waiting and often not knowing.

Within my first week of working the street, a police van pulled up driven by two on-duty members. All of a sudden, they opened the back of the van and out popped several off-duty officers sufficiently lubricated. A loud and at the time uncomfortable exchange took place between the on-duty and off-duty members. They seemed to be quite enjoying themselves and laughing loudly about the day's events. I was too new to understand and was uncomfortable about the circumstances. Fortunately, for the most part, that type of behaviour was rare, but it was clear evidence to me that alcohol was a part of the culture and at the time necessary, it seemed, to deal with the stress of policing. For myself, I did not participate in this type of de-stressing and wasn't looked on too favourably because of it. Somehow you weren't trusted if you didn't drink.

When I conducted the across-Canada interviews it was apparent that alcohol was an accepted practice within policing to de-stress, but it was obvious from the interviews that alcohol was a common problem for officers in their marriages as well. Virtually every officer and spouse I interviewed noted the struggle they had observed in themselves and/or other officers over the addictions associated with alcohol. For many it had damaging and permanent implications to their marriages as many, but not all, ended in divorce.

There is a new movement in recent years among the younger generation. While alcohol is still part of the culture, it appears not to have the same hold it once did. There does appear to be a greater emphasis on fitness so members are working out more consistently and family appears to be more important. This is good news.

A second area of addictive behaviour mentioned in the survey is sexual addiction. A few people mentioned in their interviews that they had seen officers fall prey to what is commonly called "blue fever". This is where women are attracted to the uniform and officers fall prey to the come-ons. This is very real threat to the marriage.

A few years ago I was patrolling a local bar and dance club in the south end of Calgary. I was there looking for inappropriate drunks, underage minors and just generally seeing that people were behaving themselves. It is common practice among the police and liquor establishments. I noticed that this one rather attractive young lady was beginning to follow me as I wandered through the bar, constantly talking to me. She began touching my arm, sometimes my shoulder, all the while engaging me in conversation. I started to feel quite uncomfortable about this and suggested to my partner it was time to leave. This gal followed us all the way out to our police unit. Quite honestly, I was flattered but I also didn't want this getting out of hand. I had seen other officers get sucked in and hand out their cards to these young ladies. I made my escape. Unfortunately, we received a call back to this establishment about 30 minutes later on a serious injury assault where a patron had hit another patron across the side of the head with a glass mug and sliced this guy's head for several inches with a lot of blood involved. Paramedics were called and we sorted through the witnesses and arrested the bad guy. While I am doing this, trying to stay focused on the task at hand, this young lady once again cozies up to me and almost harasses me for a number or to get together later. I am trying to conduct an investigation, arrest an offender and here she is trying to get me to play. I finally had to tell her in no uncertain terms to leave me alone, I wasn't interested.

Other officers however have gotten themselves into a whole mess of trouble over this issue and if sexual addiction was a concern they'd often fall and find their bags packed out the door by their partners. I had a partner who got caught up in womanizing and frequently would take time off work, sometimes in the middle of the shift, to meet up with an interested party. I remember one time being so angry that he'd left me during a night shift that I wasn't paying attention and blew through a red light and just missed getting hit from someone going through the green. He was married a couple of years later, but it didn't take long before I found out his marriage ended because he couldn't stop dealing with the attention of the girls.

The Servant Warrior needs to place his identity in God who has given him or her, their son-ship or daughterhood. Our identity and purpose is not found in drugs, alcohol or sexual relationships. Our marriage partner needs to be assured of our commitment to the relationship and not to the police culture or sexual conquests. Spouses and officers need to talk about these issues frankly and honestly so the relationship can be safeguarded.

Work-related Stressors

There are many work-related stressors that impact the police marriage but some I have already spoken about including hyper-vigilance, over-commitment to work and time commitments. I will focus on two general topics, one related to external stressors and the other to internal stressors. The external refers to those things which occur outside the control of the police service and relate directly to the job of policing and the other is to the stressors brought on by being part of the police service.

The main external stressor that impacts family and marriage is critical incident stress. A critical incident is an event that is so powerful that it overwhelms the normal coping ability of a normal person and has the potential to leave a first responder with scars for life. These events are typically line of duty deaths of another officer, child related death or serious injury, multiple casualties like a bus or plane crash or 9-11 type event, a failed mission where someone dies as a result or any other significant and potentially damaging event. The sights and sound, smells and touch and even taste of these events stay with the officers and first responders all their lives. They bring the damage of these things home with them and their spouses will be touched and sometimes damaged themselves by the intensity of the experience.

It has been argued that 30% of police officers will experience some form of lasting critical incident stress that lasts longer than 30 days. This could include such symptoms as interrupted sleep, intrusive dreams, increase in anger, image flashbacks, etc. The spouses will be the recipient of or experience first hand all of these symptoms from the officer. Helping spouses understand what their Servant Warrior is experiencing will help them understand that they are not the problem, so they can give them a listening and appropriate ear. Helping them to see where they may have been of help or assistance to another human being in an event that was totally out of their control may help them to experience some of what they were designed for.

It is equally important for police agencies and the officer themselves to take responsibility for their own learning in this area and understand the impact these stressors have on their own families. We as officers, have a responsibility to hear and listen to our spouses as they experience us and with humble hearts move towards meeting their needs in the midst of these issues. This does not mean to grow silent and not speak about our issues because we're afraid this will cause fear in our spouses. There are mutual ways in which we can communicate clearly our own needs and hear the needs of our spouses and adjust to their needs as well.

I heard a recent story of one young officer who had a particularly bad day. He had attended several domestic violence situations and a serious injury vehicle accident and then, just as his shift was ending, he received a call of a young man that had committed suicide. Once the scene was dealt with, he had to go and talk to the father of this young man. He shared a few tears with the father over this most distressing news and the father thanked him for his presence and the way he'd dealt with the family. As the officer was driving home to his spouse, he reflected on the day and was pretty distressed over what good he'd accomplished. He was at a low point in his career and wondered what the use was. The spouse was able to help him reflect on the day. She didn't tell him what to think but helped him to look back. He was able to identify the moment when he was able to connect with the father and though he'd brought very bad news he shared his humanity with another human and was thanked. He felt he'd been God's servant when he needed to be and brought comfort in a bad situation.

If done with thoughtfulness and caring, spouses can help an officer see his or her role as a servant warrior in a world that is not very nice and, at times, seems to be at war. This can be a significant help in deterring cumulative stress that can build up over years of dealing with one bad situation after another. Occasionally, an officer can experience a seemingly insignificant event and yet due to cumulative stress suffer a drop in performance as a result. Like the straw that breaks the camels back, the officer reacts to the final event. Spouses who are aware of Critical Incident Stress Management can assist the officer in identifying the issues at hand and getting the support and guidance he/she might need.

A work-related stressor worth commenting on is when children live with the shift worker. For couples who both work out of the house, day care is certainly a potential solution to keeping the children quiet when the officer is trying to sleep. Over the years we learned to either create a room in the basement or a bedroom with curtains that reduce light coming into the room. In both cases having a fan going creating "white" noise that drowns out the ambient noises can help with sleep patterns. Ear plugs can also be a help.Keeping the kids quiet can be a real stress on the spouse and is difficult for the children as well. Creative solutions and discussion can help in this matter.

One of the major stressors that any police officer will experience is the stressors associated directly with the internal politics of the police agency. Such things as internal affairs investigation on the officer, promotional processes at all levels of management, poor functioning teams, poor leadership, the ever going gossip stream and the occasional bad partner. All of these create stress for the officer and in most surveys, often rank highest among stressors. These things come home to the spouse usually in the form of fear, frustration and/or anger.

In my own story, the promotional process created a huge challenge for my wife and me. Because my identity was so wrapped up in my role as a detective and police officer, the rejection was very significant. I was hurt and angry and my wife received most of that, not out of anything she had done but because of how I felt treated. Promotional time is often called the silly season because of the commitment for preparation, studies and interviews that can take months to complete. Then officer and families have to deal with the emotions of the rejection (which police officers tend not to handle very well) or the celebration and excitement of the promotion. If promoted, there is the inevitable change that once again impacts the family.

You can't be in policing for very long without finding yourself being investigated through internal affairs because of a citizen's complaint. I had the misfortune of being charged with assault on a would-be break and enter suspect after we pulled him through the broken window that he created. He managed to find a justice of the peace that would take his complaint and Internal Affairs was forced to issue a court appearance on me for assault. Fortunately, the information was sent to an out-of-town crown prosecutor who stayed the charges against me because there were insufficient grounds and the fact I had a legal arrest. That process took three months. It was a frightening time in particular for my spouse because she was seriously concerned about security and my career. What would we do if I lost my job? This was a real concern to both of us. Learning about the internal affairs process and being kept informed was extremely helpful to me and ultimately to my wife. It helped to minimize the fear. It is so important for the Servant Warrior to include his or her spouse in the conversations during these times. Many times, fear of the unknown causes more stress than the actual event. Keeping the spouse informed is essential.

Sometimes when an investigation takes place, the officer is suspended from duty until the investigation is complete and charges either laid or the officer is reinstated. This is a very stressful time for the officer and the spouse. Uncertainty abounds and sometimes the police service doesn't provide all the information about what is happening to the officer. This creates huge fear and frustration and often leads to anger towards the department. It is at times like this that faith is so helpful. The word faith means the assurance of things hoped for and the conviction of what is not yet seen. When the servant warrior places hope and faith in the One who has called him or her, they can be assured that even if things don't work out the way they thought it should or would, the One who loves the servant warrior will turn all things to good. He is a God of Justice and justice usually prevails even if it is not seen for some time. With faith there is an awareness that sometimes the most difficult times in our lives turn out to be the greatest milestone some years down the road. Change occurs and it is good, although at the time it can be unbelievably painful. Faith allows us as servant warriors to walk in the assurance that God has our best at heart, so that we can say with confidence, "What can man do to me?" Really!

During a brainstorming session I held to discuss family priorities within policing, a major issue that came up for the families was leadership, good or bad. If the leader has a servant warrior attitude often this is very good for the families. The leader understands the importance of family and marriage and makes concessions on the part of the officer and his family and makes life generally easier. If however, the leader is more autocratic this can cause great consternation for the families' shifts often get changed to meet the needs of the service rather than the family and the family has absolutely no say. In policing an officer can be moved around without much input from one community to the next or from one division to the next. Without input the officers get very disgruntled and the family usually pays the price. If the leadership takes an interest in the officer and provides opportunity for meaningful work, then the family benefits because the officer is far happier in his work and is energized by it. For marriages or partnerships and family, good leadership can make all the difference in the world.

So as you can see, this is only a portion of the work-related stressors that can play into the Servant Warrior in his role at home. Faith in God can help reduce much of the stress associated with these situations if we as servant warriors are willing to trust God with the result and seek Him for our responses to these stressors.

Communication

As in any lasting and rewarding relationship, communication is the key. In the interviews I conducted, the officers and spouses mentioned over and over again that they were able to improve their relationships by learning how to effectively communicate with each other even through the occasional fight. Several had to learn the hard way and I must include myself in this. One of the more effective ways of communicating on the street is to use anger to get what is needed or necessary. It is easy to transfer that home. Though the officer may not intend to speak with his spouse in a tone of anger, it is difficult not to sound angry. This puts the partner on the defensive right away and leads to disagreements. As I said earlier, using cop techniques at home seldom works.

Another issue for officers and partners in relationships is the withdrawal aspect of coming home from duty. Often officers will come home and vegetate in front of the television or the computer and zone out. Often the partner has to stand in front of the television to get the officer's attention. It seems the officer has no energy left when he or she arrives home. Communication is difficult when one party doesn't want to play and at best you get a grunt of agreement or acknowledgement. I was quite famous for this around our home. When I came home, I'd sit in front of the computer as a way of not having to think. This helped my wife to feel valued and cherished......NOT. Many times she stood in front of me and looked at me for some time until I acknowledged her presence. This did not work well for us and particularly for me. I'm not a particularly quick learner apparently and after a few good fights leaving Deborah feeling very misunderstood, we came to an agreement that when I was working day shift in particular, she would let me come home and grab a fifteen minute nap but then I had to come and engage her so she could share her day with me. Adult conversation was needed and necessary for her as we had young children at the time. This nap also helped me to recover and have the energy to re-engage with my kids and my wife.

One area that used to drive my wife and apparently other spouses a bit stir-crazy was when we would get together with another couple. Most often the conversation would get around to work and usually this conversation ended up negative and critical of the service or other members. Dr. Kevin Gilmartin puts it bluntly. While I won't use the language he used, you get the picture. They are all the backside of donkeys and it's all inaccurate!!! This negativity has an impact in communication with our spouses. As servant warriors at home we would stand ourselves in a far better place with our families if we would stick to more positive topics. One of my favorite verses that I need to remind myself of regularly is found in Philippians 4:8:

> Finally brothers, whatever is true, whatever is honorable, whatever is just, whatever is pure, whatever is lovely, whatever is commendable – if there is any moral excellence, if there is any praise – dwell on these things.....and the God of peace will be with you.

This verse could help us cynical negative cops a lot if we practiced it daily. Communication with our spouses would be much more pleasurable for us and them. The servant warrior sees enough garbage out in the world but at home there needs to be an effort to speak what is truth in love with a focus on the more positive aspects of our family and friends.

With the list of things that have been identified by others as issues in their marriages, it can seem overwhelmingly negative and I don't want to end this book in this fashion. There is significant hope for all officers in their home life. It is not the intent of this book to address the police marriage. God willing that will come later but I want to leave some principles that have worked for my own marriage and have worked for others as well. These principles can be laid out specifically in the use of two words.... LOVE and RESPECT.

Love and Respect

Over the past ten years as the chaplain for the Calgary Police Service, I have had the privilege of giving marriage preparation counseling and performing these marriages under God. My practice is to have three sessions where we discuss a number of issues related to police marriage including the subjects that I listed previously. These have an impact on the marriage and they need to be aware of and prepare for these issues in their marriage. The fourth session is spent going over the marriage that God intended in the Bible. The two words that speak volumes in the Bible about how couples are to treat each other are Love and Respect. Without these two words working in the relationship, the relationship is doomed especially in a police world where marriages don't survive well.

The most succinct verses on the marriage that God desires is found in Ephesians 5: 22 – 33:

> Wives, submit to your own husbands as to the
> Lord, for the husband is head of the wife as also
> Christ is head of the church. He is the savior of
> the body. Now as the church submits to Christ
> so wives should submit to their husbands in
> everything. Husbands love your wives, just as

also Christ loved the church and gave Himself for her, to make her holy, cleansing her in the washing of water by the Word. He did this to present the church to himself in splendor, without spot or wrinkle or any such thing but holy and blameless. In the same way, husbands should love their wives as their own bodies. He who loves his wife loves himself. For no one ever hates his own flesh, but provides and cares for it, just as Christ does for the church since we are members of His body.

For this reason a man will leave his father and mother and be joined to his wife, and the two will become one flesh.

This mystery is profound, but I am talking about Christ and the church. . **To sum up, each one of you is to love his wife as himself and the wife is to respect her husband.**

In an effort to be politically correct, I need to say to the female officers and spouses out there that this needs to be understood in context. First and foremost, husbands and wives are seen as equals under God's eyes. They are sons and daughters and there is no distinction. There are those who have used this passage as an excuse to force women into submission. This is completely unbiblical and has no support in scripture. If fact, if a husband mistreats his spouse in any way, his own prayers and communication with God will not heard. He will not be on God's good side.

The most important thing to see here is that the husband is to unconditionally love his wife and the wife is to unconditionally respect her husband.

I am now learning to dance. For many years I was terrified of dancing and my meager attempts to dance met with miserable failure and embarrassment. In fact, when I was a school resource officer we were to go to a graduation banquet with the recent grads. Deborah came to the school during a lunch hour because the school brought in some dance instructors to teach the students to dance. I agreed to participate. I lasted ten minutes before I threw up my hands in frustration because I wasn't getting it and was embarrassing myself. Deborah was telling me what to do and it wasn't working. She was getting frustrated and was trying to lead me. Well in dance that just doesn't work, so I quit. I got up the courage after our daughter and son-in-law bought us dance lessons in a smaller setting. The instructor was excellent and went at a pace that I could follow and helped me with my steps and in my leading. He made it very clear however to the ladies that they were to follow the lead of the man. If you did not do that it would lead to disaster. His words were, "Men, you lead, but it is your job to make the ladies shine."

If you read the passage I just gave in that context, you understand what marriage is. Men are to lead as under Christ but it is their job to make the ladies shine, to become a person of splendor and beauty. Men are to serve their wives literally as servant warriors willing to give their lives for the sake of our ladies. I mentioned what unconditional love is and servant leadership in a previous chapter. This is the same kind of love a husband is to have for his spouse. When I explain this to the fiancés of the officers I do weddings for, they get it. They know that they will not be submitting themselves to a person who will use his leadership to harm but rather to help her become all that she is to be.

When I first started talking to male officers about their role as husbands, I would put the pressure on them because the Bible makes it clear that the man is the only one in the marriage relationship that is called to unconditionally love his wife. This is the love that God has for all of us. It is unconditional. The wife is not called to unconditionally love her husband. She is called to love her husband with an affection and friendship. Unconditional love is expressed in the same way as described in an earlier chapter. It is patient, kind, doesn't envy, boast or get conceited. It is polite, selfless and praises the other without a record of wrong. It celebrates the good and rejoices in truth. These are the actions of love. It isn't based on a feeling that comes and goes but rather on a commitment to behave in this manner towards our spouses.

For most women, love is a natural thing. They naturally nurture and have compassion for their loved ones. For men, generally, this is something that must be learned. Respect is what comes naturally for men. We live in a world of respect or disrespect. The most important thing we give our fellow servant warriors is respect. We seek that same respect both from our peers but also from our fathers. We as men desire love as well but it is often expressed most within the context of respect. For a woman, this is not as natural but something they must learn.

As an example, I think of the years I spent working in the high schools. If two guys decided to have a fight over something, they would have the fight, cheered on by their peers, then, not always but frequently, these two would become friends or at least good acquaintances after the year was up. Why? Because they developed respect for each other. They stood up to each other and earned a respect for the other. Girls on the other hand, were brutal. If they got into a fight, that fight would last forever. They would rarely if ever become friends and often the dislike would carry on even after high school. It was an interesting observation.

Respect is important and natural for men and love is important and natural for women. That is why the scriptures teach us that women are to unconditionally respect their husband

and husbands are to unconditionally love their wives. Neither is natural for the other but it is something they must learn and depend on their relationship with Jesus to accomplish. Notice that the wife is to submit to the husband **AS** unto Christ. Men are to love their wives **AS** Christ loved the church. Jesus is our example in both situations. Jesus submitted himself to his Father's will and out of love for the church he gave himself up for its sake.

Many will ask the question, "What if I'm in an abusive situation?" In either case, male or female, we are to do our part to love and respect the other person. However, that does not mean you continue to put up with the abuse. Every effort must be made to stop the abuse, including leaving for a period of time if necessary in order to seek the help required for both parties to learn to live well with each other. Most people are not evil-willed people. They don't get up in the morning and say, "How can I make my spouse's life miserable today?" Many do have significant issues that seem to rise up out the past that impact marriage quite significantly if not violently. These must be dealt with, usually with the help of others including professional counselors or therapists.

The best part is that nearly all of us, particularly in the law enforcement world, are in fact good-willed people who desire the best for ourselves, our loved ones and others. We usually wake up in the morning with the intent of doing something that will have a positive impact on others, especially our families. I think of the prayer I recently found:

Dear Lord,

So far today, I've done all right. I haven't gossiped, haven't lost my temper, haven't been

greedy, grumpy, nasty, selfish, or over indulgent.
I'm very thankful for that.

But, in a few minutes, God, I'm going to get out
of bed. And from then on, I'm probably going to
need a lot more help.

This is how most of us crawl out of bed. We intend to do
good in the lives of others and in our family. We are good-willed
people who struggle with the reality of marriage and relationships. It is very important that the servant warrior and spouse
remember that when they approach their marriage. Both of you
are good-willed people and intend good for each other not evil.
Unfortunately, even good-willed people become a little crazy
when they relate to each other.

In a great book by Dr. Emerson Eggerichs, *Love and Respect*,
the concept of the crazy cycle is introduced. This is what
happens when partners don't practice love or respect to each
other. Eggerichs explains it this way; without love – she reacts
– without respect – he reacts – without love and the crazy cycle
begins.[23] Sometimes it feels like we are desperately on this crazy
cycle and we will never get off. I witnessed this in my own marriage just recently. For some time I'd been really quite in love
with my wife, however we had a discussion that revolved around
whether I felt desired in the marriage. She made a comment to
me that I found quite disrespectful, though she did not intend it
that way. I reacted to her statement without a loving response to
which she reacted again with another statement that dug deeper.
Now I was hurt and reacted. These reactions got worse because I
did not talk to her about how I felt disrespected. For weeks after
that I continued to build a case that she did not desire me and
ultimately did not respect my need. I built a reservoir against her
based on a complete lie. Some of it was true but most of it was

not and I began to treat her in unloving, curt ways that caused her to feel very unloved and our crazy cycle spun for several weeks. I must confess that most of this was my fault because she had no intention of hurting me. She was talking to me about her own struggles and I did not acknowledge what was happening for her but chose to be offended and feel disrespected. Finally, I could stand it no longer and had to apologize for my poor choice in behaviour and repair the relationship. Fortunately she is a gracious woman and she forgave me and we were able to return to a healthier relationship with each other.

As husband and wife, our commitment to learn to love and respect each other is probably the most important attribute in marriage. We must remain committed to the learning process. It was our commitment to our relationship with God that salvaged our relationship. Because I was committed to God, I literally cried out to him to give me the strength to learn what I needed about Deborah so that I could remain married. Faith was a huge part of our marriage even surviving. Fortunately both of us were committed to God and to each other and our vow to learn about what our needs were.

Another book that we found particularly helpful in our marriage and the learning process was *His Needs, Her Needs* by Willard Harley. Harley describes in detail ten needs that he identified over the years he has been doing marriage counseling. These needs are: affection, sexual fulfillment, conversation, recreational companionship, honesty and openness, attractiveness of spouse, domestic support, family commitment and finally admiration.[24]

When I went back and reviewed the work we'd done together to determine each other's needs and learn how to meet those needs, our needs were quite different except in two areas. My needs were admiration, sexual fulfillment, honesty and openness, recreational companionship and family commitment. Deborah's were conversation, honesty and openness, affection, financial support and family commitment. Knowing each others needs in a more concrete way helped us to learn what was needed to meet those needs in each other. For Deborah and I, it was interesting how meeting one of our needs helped to meet the other's needs. For example, I needed recreational companionship and she needed conversation. We took an inventory of things we like to do and as a result found some things in common that we could do that surprised us. For us, one of those things was horses and riding. We began to pursue this. As a result, it led to a great deal of conversation which helped to meet Deb's need. We were enjoying horses together and this gave us time and space to converse with each other.

My encouragement to all servant warriors is to take their home life seriously. It needs to be the second most important relationship you have apart from your relationship with the God who has called you into your identity, purpose, roles and the relationships you have with others, including the one you chose to marry. Faith can have a huge impact on the marriage. God desires that we have a strong marriage and live as an example of what His love is like towards us and the world He loves. The definition of success in this life is to have developed strong relationships with the ones we love especially our spouses, children and friends. These are the things that will go forward with us into heaven. Nothing physical that we have made or bought will go with us. Faith in a God who loves us and them will strengthen us if we trust God to help us in these important relationships.

May God bless you in your journey as a servant warrior. May God Himself give you the grace to be all that you can be for Him. He has identified you as His adopted son or daughter, a citizen of another kingdom. He has given you a special calling and role in a broken world both as a servant to His people and a warrior who stands in the gap against the evil one. He has called all of us into a leadership role that exemplifies Jesus' servant leadership. He has promised to be with us and shown us how to care for ourselves and those around us. He has provided us with meaningful relationships in which we learn more about His love for us. All of this is based on faith in a Creator who loves us deeply. Faith in policing has a profound role. Blessed are those who live by faith. Blessed are the peacemakers for they will be called the sons of God.

References

(Endnotes)

1   Emotional Survival for Law Enforcement; a Guide for Officers and Family; Dr. Kevin Gilmartin Pg, 77 Published by E-S Press (January 2002)

2   Sharpening the Warriors Edge: The Psychology & Science of Training (Paperback) by Bruce K. Siddle (Author) PPCT Research Publications; 1 edition (October 1, 1995)

3   Finishing Well; What people who "really live" do differently. By Bob Buford pg
Copyright 2004 published by Integrity Publishing

4   God's Word for Peace Officers, Tactical Edition Bible; published by Peace officers ministries, Inc. and God's Word for the Nations Bible Society; Pg 24

5   The Servant, A simple story about the true essence of Leadership; James C. Hunter
Copyright 1998, published by Prima Publishing – Random House

6   The Servant, Pg 100

7   The Servant, Pg 124

8   The Servant, Pg 125

9   Jon Hooper "I am a Warrior" http://www.nleomf.org/TheMemorial/tributes/poetry/poetry_hooper.htm

10 The Way of the Wild Heart: A Map for the Masculine Journey John Eldredge. Copyright 2006 published by Thomas Nelson Inc.

11 Spirit Warriors: Strategies for the Battles Christian Men and Women Face Every Day; Stu Webber - pg 63 Copyright 2001 published by Multnomah Publishers Inc.

12 Chris Butler – Interview and submission

13 Why Courage Matters: John McAin and Marshall Salter. Copyright 2004 published by Random House

14 Spirit Warriors; pg

15 Spirit Warriors; pg

16 Chief Mark Field; The Ethic Role Call, Summer & Fall 2001

17 Chief Mark Field; The Ethic Role Call, Summer & Fall 2001, Part 2

18 The Servant; James Hunter, Pg. 89

19 The Seven Habits of Highly Effective People; Restoring the character ethic copyright by Steven Covey; Pg 151

20 http://www.crosswalk.com/11536752/ Author Michael Warden

21 Spiritual Direction; Wisdom for the Long Walk of Faith by
    Henri Nouwen - copyright 2006. Published by HarperCollins
    Publishers, New York (Page 119)

22 Spiritual Direction (pg 119)

23 Love and Respect. Copyright 2004 by Emerson Eggerichs
    published by Integrity Publishers, Pg 5

24 His Needs Her Needs; Building an affair-proof marriage.
    By Willard Harley, copyright 2001. Published by Fleming H
    Revel of Baker Book House Company

CPSIA information can be obtained
at www.ICGtesting.com
Printed in the USA
LVOW12s0926120117

520500LV00001B/19/P